Free to Minister

Dennis A. Vauk

Back Cover Photo by Amber Vauk

ISBN: 978-0-6151-6117-4

Contact: DennisVauk@aol.com

Additional copies of this book can be ordered at: www.lulu.com

Acknowledgements

I would like to thank my wife and partner in the ministry, Donna, for her constant support, encouragement and inspiration.

I also acknowledge all those that have paved the way before me in ministry, trained me, and helped to show me the way. Special thanks to Mosy and Gloria Madugba of Ministers' Prayer Network who have shown us a model of Christian leadership.

Much gratitude and love go the pastoral team and my brothers and sisters at Calvary Community Church and especially to our Executive Pastor, Jeff McGee. Jeff has been a source of wise counsel for us as we started out in ministry. Thanks to Jeff and also to Sehoy Meeks for their assistance in editing this manuscript. Thanks to Evan Vauk for his help in layout and publishing of this book.

There are also two other ministers of the Gospel that taught me many valuable lessons that have become a part of what I believe and teach. Rod Parsley, pastor of World Harvest Church, shared with me the truth that we must have Christ's character to walk in His authority. Rick Joyner, Founder of MorningStar Fellowship Church, revealed many truths to me about the spiritual battle we are in through his book, The Final Quest. These truths have become a vital part of the teachings shared in this book.

Dennis Vauk
June, 2007

Dedication

This book is dedicated to the readers of this book and fellow workers in the Lord. May you be encouraged to step out in ministry after reading this book, do mighty exploits for our Lord, and cause much damage to the works of darkness in the world.

Contents

Foreword

Having led a strong global apostolic and prophetic movement for the past 11 years, I can easily identify with every bit of the message in this book, which is very timely as of today. When a seasoned farmer who regularly plants various species of the apple tree sees an apple fruit, it is easy for him to identify its specific type.

As I read the summary of the entire content of Dennis Vauk's *Free to Minister,* several warm feelings surged through my spirit man. First, I was excited to know another man who has escaped the crippling effort of the old wine skin and has transformed to the new with a clear understanding of the essence of the current Apostolic and Prophetic reformative move by the Holy Spirit. As I travel within the larger body of Christ around the world, I discover with some uneasiness that a large majority of Church folks are yet to catch up with where God is. He has divine times and seasons assigned to various moves and works of the Holy Spirit on earth. Every generation has a specific divine mandate to fulfill. Secondly, he shared elaborately many other valuable truths in this book, that I began to think of an alternative, more comprehensive title for it, which would encompass and totally represent the other revelations and teachings in it. Thirdly, I was excited that another relevant and straight-to-the-point book for this divine season is made available to the body of Christ.

We are right in the midst of one of the most powerful reformative moves of the Holy Spirit in the history of the Church on earth. Free to Minister will provide relevant knowledge of what the move is all about to every honest inquirer. It will equip any Christian who wants to be actively involved, inform every Pastor who feels insecure to let go of the old order of doing church work, and embrace the original apostolic pattern of the church with its kingdom emphasis. It will encourage every believer to serve God within the Body of Christ as Christ originally intended.

The result of the aforementioned will be a stronger church, more powerful manifestations of the miracles and signs by individual church members, and an unprecedented growth of the church after the apostolic pattern. I appreciate the courage of Dennis Vauk and his heart of obedience to the Holy Spirit to write this timely book. I do recommend it to the Body of Christ worldwide with delight and much prayer.

Rev. Mosy U. Madugba
International Coordinator, Ministers Prayer Network - Worldwide
Melbourne, Florida
July 2005

1

Introduction

God is reforming and transforming His church from a hierarchical structure with only the clergy doing ministry work to a church where the body is doing the work of the ministry. God defined the structure he wanted for the church and how he wanted the church to function in Ephesians 4:11-16.

And He Himself gave some to be apostles, some prophets, some evangelists, and some pastors and teachers, for the equipping of the saints for the work of ministry, for the edifying of the body of Christ, till we all come to the unity of the faith and of the knowledge of the Son of God, to a perfect man, to the measure of the stature of the fullness of Christ; that we should no longer be children, tossed to and fro and carried about with every wind of doctrine, by the trickery of men, in the cunning craftiness of deceitful plotting, but, speaking the truth in love, may grow up in all things into Him who is the head-- Christ— from whom the whole body, joined and knit together by what every joint supplies, according to the effective working by which every part does its share, causes growth of the body for the edifying of itself in love. (Ephesians 4:11-16)

Note that the purpose of the five-fold ministry – the apostles, prophets, evangelists, pastors and teachers - is to equip the saints to do the work of ministry. For many years we have had a separation of the clergy and the laity – with the clergy doing all the ministry work. But this was a departure from the original structure that Jesus desired as noted in His instructions in Paul's letter to the Ephesians. Since Martin Luther began the reformation, God has continued to reform his church. What we see is a continuing unfolding of God's pattern for the church as he sends wave after wave of reformation to prepare His bride, the church, for his coming. In this study we will explore how the body is being purified and released to do the work of the ministry.

> **When we speak of the Body of Christ being released to minister, we are speaking about a revolution in the way the Church sees its mission.**

"Do not try to teach others to do what you, yourself, are not doing. Reformation is not just a doctrine. True reformation only comes from union with the Savior. When you are yoked with Christ, carrying the burdens that He gives you, He will be with you and carry them for you. You can only do His work when you are doing it with Him, not just for Him. Only the Spirit can beget that which is Spirit. If you are yoked with Him you will do nothing for the sake of politics or history. Anything that you do because of political pressures, or opportunities, will only lead you to the end of your true ministry. The things that are done in an effort to make history will at best confine your accomplishments to history, and you will fail to impact eternity. If you do not live what you preach to others you disqualify yourself from the high calling of God...." The Final Quest by Rick Joyner, Morning Star Publications, Copyright 1996 (page 101)

When we speak of the Body of Christ being released to minister, we are speaking about a revolution in the way the Church sees its mission. To see this reformation through, God has released a new breed of ministers in these last 20 years – apostles and prophets. In the quote above from Rick Joyner's book, he shows us that the intent of these ministers that are reforming the Church is key to their success. They must be about the Lord's business and doing it with Him, not out of self-promotion. In this book, we will discuss the key characteristics of apostles and prophets that God is releasing. We will also address how the enemy is using trickery and deceitful plotting by some of his agents to keep the Body as children – unable to minister as Christ wants them to.   Since some of these agents may call themselves apostles or prophets to justify their control over the people, it is important to be able to see the true from the false. Finally we will discuss how important relationships are in supporting one another in the body if the church is to grow up into all things that Christ has commissioned us to do.

2

The Five-Fold Ministry

And He Himself gave some to be apostles, some prophets, some evangelists, and some pastors and teachers, for the equipping of the saints for the work of ministry, for the edifying of the body of Christ, till we all come to the unity of the faith and of the knowledge of the Son of God, to a perfect man, to the measure of the stature of the fullness of Christ...(Ephesians 4:11-13)

The work of the five-fold ministry (apostles, prophets, evangelists, pastors, and teachers) is like the farming process. The role of the apostle is like the pioneer. He cuts back the brush, clears out the trees, and fights off any hostile attack of the enemy. He makes it safe to farm. In the same way, the apostle goes into new territory and prepares it for the advancement of the Church. This may be going to unreached people groups. This is the area of ministry that we often call missionary. It could also mean going into unreached areas of ministry that have not previously been explored.

The prophet is like the plowman. The plowman uncovers the earth in big chunks. He determines the direction of the crop rows. In the same way, the prophet points the direction of the church.

The teacher is like the harrow. The harrow takes what the plowmen have turned over in big chunks and breaks it down into smaller pieces of soil that are good for planting. Similarly, the teacher takes what God has declared through the apostle and prophets and establishes the doctrine - the teachings that edify the church.

The pastor is like the farmer who plants and tends the crop. He makes sure it gets the right amount of water. He fights off any intruders that might harm it. He kills off any weeds that might try to strangle the crops or prevent the light from coming in and limiting growth of the crop. He fertilizes. He activates the crop in order to bring it completely to ripeness and ensures that the crop will be bountiful. In the same way, a pastor tends to his flock. He feeds them the word of God. He protects them from those who may try to manipulate them or divert them from their path.

The evangelist is like the harvester. The harvester takes in the crop once it has been tended and brought to full maturity. Similarly, the evangelist is especially gifted to bring people into the kingdom. It is each member's duty to plant seeds and water them. The evangelist helps them bring in the harvest.

What are the Key Characteristics of Apostles and Prophets?

And God has appointed these in the church: first apostles, second prophets, third teachers, after that miracles, then gifts of healings, helps, administrations, varieties of tongues. (1 Corinthians 12:28)

Apostles are first in Order: Paul says that God appointed *first apostles, second prophets.* The word translated first comes from the Greek *proton*, which means firstly (in time, place, or order). To establish the church in new territory, the apostolic anointing is the first, primary anointing.

Breakthrough Prayers: In God's army the apostles are the marine expeditionary forces. As an expeditionary force is assigned to break through enemy lines and establish a base camp for the rest of the forces, so the apostles break through the enemy's lines and establish foundation for the church.

Militancy: As an expeditionary force they are ruthless in attacking the enemy, whether it is the devil working through religious spirits in the church or other worldly ways. In this role, they exhibit the characteristic that Jesus showed us when He cleansed the temple. The apostles are sent by God to break through entrenched positions of the enemy, and cleanse the church of them to allow God's glory to be manifested.

Show the Love of the Father: What is the apostle first in? Jesus says, *"By this all will know that you are My disciples, if you have love for one another."* (John 13:35) So, the first anointing of any prophet, the first anointing of any apostle, the first anointing of any minister must be that they have love for one another. The apostle, above anything else, must be able to demonstrate the love of God to others. If he does not demonstrate above all else the love of God, then he is not truly an apostle. Jesus tells us to *"Beware of false prophets, who come to you in sheep's clothing, but inwardly they are ravenous wolves. You will know them by their fruits. Do men gather grapes from thornbushes or figs from thistles?"* (Matthew 7:15-16) A true prophet, a true apostle, a true pastor, a true teacher, or evangelist will demonstrate that fruit of the spirit by which Jesus says that we will know he is a disciple, "that you have love for one another." If that fruit is not present, then we are to "beware" of them.

> **The apostle, above anything else, must be able to demonstrate the love of God to others.**

Paul emphasized the same principle. After stating that God has given *"first apostles, second prophets"* in 1 Corinthians 12:31 he states, *"But earnestly desire the best gifts. And yet I show you a more excellent way."* The more excellent way Paul was talking about was "love" as he detailed in Chapter 13.

Though I speak with the tongues of men and of angels, but have not love, I have become sounding brass or a clanging cymbal. (1 Corinthians 13:1)

If a person goes forth claiming to be an apostle or prophet, but does not have love; he is just a clanging cymbal. He's just making noise to attract attention to himself and his ministry. He cannot make an impact for the Kingdom of God without love.

Apostles provide foundation to the Church through their God given anointing to build.

For we are God's fellow workers; you are God's field, you are God's building. According to the grace of God which was given to me, as a wise master builder I have laid the foundation and another builds on it. But let each one take heed how he builds on it. (1 Corinthians 3:9-10)

> **True apostles and prophets always work together to provide foundation for the church, rather than separately to build up their own kingdoms.**

Now, therefore, you are no longer strangers and foreigners, but fellow citizens with the saints and members of the household of God, having been built on the foundation of the apostles and prophets, Jesus Christ Himself being the chief corner stone, in whom the whole building, being joined together, grows into a holy temple in the Lord, in whom you also are being built together for a dwelling place of God in the Spirit. (Ephesians 2:19-22)

A critical factor is that they not only can build, but they build where God wants them to and according to the blueprint that God gives. As the foundation of a building supports the rest of the building and determines its stability, so the apostles and prophets provide the same foundational support to the church. As in a building, the foundation is first in order. So, with the church, the apostolic and prophetic anointing must be first in order for the church to be built on a proper foundation. They provide foundational support to the church through manifesting on Earth that which God is declaring in heaven. An apostle, with a prophet, discerns the mind of Christ for His church, both locally and globally. This anointing to build the Church according to God's blueprint is the distinct characteristic of the apostle and prophet.

Teamwork, Networking: In building, the apostle and prophet establish doctrine that defines a new order. *"And they continued steadfastly in the apostles' doctrine."* (Acts 2:42) The Jews who were converted on the day of Pentecost did not continue in the old Jewish order, but followed the doctrine the apostles taught. This doctrine was not something they made up, but it was that which was received from Jesus. In the same way, modern apostles and prophets hear the Word of God and establish it in the Earth.

There needs to be a partnership between apostles and prophets. The prophet is especially gifted to hear the voice of God. The apostle is gifted to build this into the earth. That is how the Church is built on the foundation of the apostles and prophets. Not just the apostles working by themselves... not just the prophets working by themselves, but the apostles and prophets working together to hear the will of God and build it in His Church. So, if someone claims to be an apostle or prophet, but is a lone ranger, outside of relationship with other apostles and prophets, he is not the true thing. True apostles and prophets always work together to provide foundation for the church, rather than separately to build up their own kingdoms.

Attitude of a servant: According to Pastor Cosmas Ilechukwu, servant leadership means "empowering others to fulfill the purpose of God for their lives. This involves coming alongside the other person and offering any possible assistance that will help the person discover and develop his gifts and use them in the service of the Lord. It is enabling others to fulfill the mandate of God upon their lives. The focus of servant leadership is the people to be cared for and not merely the job to be accomplished. This does not mean that a servant leader is not an achiever; it means that he does not see people as mere tools to be used to achieve his objectives." Leadership is not about how many people serve you, but about how many people you serve. (Mosy Madugba, Understanding the New Prophetic and Apostolic Move of God)

Paul said *"And I will not be burdensome to you; for I do not seek yours, but you. For the children ought not to lay up for the parents, but the parents for the children. And I will very gladly spend and be spent for your souls."* (2 Corinthians 12:14-15) This expressed Paul's desire to serve the people, to "lay up" something for them. Even though apostles and prophets were appointed in the "first" position, a foundational position, this does not make them better than other parts of the ministry. As the apostolic and prophetic ministries are a foundational part of the church, they function in a supporting position, even when they provide leadership to the Church. It is worldly to think that leadership means lording over the people. Jesus provided the example of leading with a servant's mentality. An apostle or prophet given by Jesus will have the same servant character as Jesus. The apostles and prophets do not sit at the top of the church being supported by it. The apostles and prophets are at the foundation of the church, supplying support to it. Paul, an apostle, said he would *"gladly spend and be spent for your souls."* This is the character of an apostle.

Are sent forth in power: When Jesus sent the 12 apostles out, he commanded them: "*Heal the sick, cleanse the lepers, raise the dead, cast out demons.*" (Matthew 10:8) Jesus was telling them to go out and do the same things He had done. This was also true of the apostles who were added after the original 12. Paul said, *"Truly the signs of an apostle were accomplished among you with all perseverance, in signs and wonders and mighty deeds."* (2 Corinthians 12:12) As apostles are sent to break through certain barriers, break into certain areas that the church has not been able to penetrate previously, there needs to be a special anointing. Jesus told us "*Unless you people see signs and wonders, you will by no means believe.*" (John 4:48) So signs and wonders are given so that people may believe in order to advance the Kingdom of God. So, in the name of Jesus, he does the same things Jesus does. These signs done in Jesus' authority and character do not glorify the apostle, but glorify Jesus who sent him.

Called and anointed by Jesus Christ: In Ephesians 4:11, Paul says *"And He Himself gave some to be apostles...".* The apostle and prophet do not designate themselves or get promoted to that office. They are called by God, and given to the church. Paul described himself as *"an apostle (not from men nor through man, but through*

Jesus Christ and God the Father who raised Him from the dead)" (Galatians 1:1).   This characteristic of an apostle or prophet is foundational. Without a true calling, there will be no manifestation of signs and wonders, no breakthrough, no attitude of a servant, but what is revealed is an individual who desires to manipulate and control people by usurping authority that is not truly his – a satrap.

> **A satrap (who may call himself an apostle or prophet) will be concerned with selfishly promoting himself, which leads to "confusion and every evil thing."**

A true apostle or prophet can be distinguished from a satrap by his fruit. A satrap (who may call himself an apostle or prophet) will be concerned with selfishly promoting himself, which leads to *"confusion and every evil thing,"* (James 3:16) while a true apostle or prophet will be concerned with fulfilling the purposes of God and exhibit His character of love.

Apostles and prophets are gifts to the body. These gifts are different, but not more important than pastors, teachers, and evangelists. So, one does not get promoted from pastor to apostle or prophet. An apostle is not a promotion to a governing position. There will be some who will try to assume the title of apostle in order to assert themselves into a position of ruling over people. They will try to assert themselves as a type of protestant pope. This was not what Jesus gave an apostle or prophet for. He gave them to serve the church and to give their life for the church, not to be a lord over it. The apostle and prophet are gifts to the body to support the body of Christ and build it up, along with the gifts of the pastor, teacher and evangelist, into the head – which is Christ.

3

Purification for Ministry

His intention was the perfecting and the full equipping of the saints (His consecrated people), [that they should do] the work of the ministering toward building up Christ's body (the church), (Ephesians 4:12 Amplified Bible)

The five-fold ministry is given to equip the saints for the work of ministry. What exactly does it mean to equip someone to do ministry? Often times in the church we train people to do tasks and call that equipping. But, I have found that equipping and edifying is best done by introducing people to and building them up in the Lord of the work, rather than concentrating on the work of the Lord. In this season, we can only do the work of the Lord if we intimately know the Lord of the work. Once people are in an intimate relationship with the Lord, the work (ministry) will flow from that relationship.

The process of **perfecting and full equipping** of the saints is one of allowing the Father to cleanse and repeatedly prune (**purify**) us.

Any branch in Me that does not bear fruit [that stops bearing] He cuts away (trims off, takes away); and He cleanses and repeatedly prunes every branch that continues to bear fruit, to make it bear more and richer and more excellent fruit. (John 15:2 Amplified Bible)

The Lord will prune us of every worldly way.

The church today is living in worldly ways. We are acting worldly if we are more concerned with our programs that support our ministry than His praise. A pastor is worldly if he tries to rule by intimidation instead of leading by inspiration. The church member is worldly if, when someone falls, we seek condemnation instead of restoration. Leaders in the church are worldly if they are more concerned with position and power than doing the will of God. We have brought worldly principles into the church and too often run the church by them. They represent the ways of the world, not the ways of God.

Today the call of the apostles and prophets is taken from Revelation 18:1-4.

After these things I saw another angel coming down from heaven, having great authority, and the earth was illuminated with his glory. And he cried mightily with a loud voice, saying, "Babylon the great is fallen, is fallen, and has become a dwelling place of demons, a prison for every foul spirit, and a cage for every unclean and hated bird! "For all the nations have drunk of the wine of the wrath of her fornication, the kings of the earth have committed fornication with her, and the merchants of the earth have become rich through the abundance of her luxury." And I heard another voice from heaven saying, "Come out of her, my people, lest you share in her sins, and lest you receive of her plagues."

> **The message to come out of Babylon is not sent to the sinners, but it is sent to the saints.**

They are referring to Babylon, a dwelling place of demons, a prison for every foul spirit, and they say to God's people: *"Come out of her, my people."* The message to come out of Babylon is not sent to the sinners, but it is sent to the saints: *"Come out of her, my people,"* come out of Babylon, *"lest you share in her sins, and lest you receive of her plagues."* We are called to come out of these worldly ways and enter the Kingdom of the Lord. We must leave Babylon and follow the Lord. What does it mean to follow the Lord today? He is calling us to reform, reconfigure, and re-structure the church out of these worldly ways into the structure ordained by God. Paul details the correct leadership structure of the church in Ephesians 4:11-13.

So we are challenged to come out of worldly ways and build the church into the body of Christ, unified in the faith, coming up to the measure of the stature of the fullness of Christ. To do that, we must reject the worldly structure in which one individual sets himself up as the head and the only source to the local body. We embrace a church structure where a plurality of leadership - apostles, prophets, and teachers, as well as the traditional evangelists and pastors - equips the body. This leadership will equip and train the body for the work of ministry. Anything less than that is not fulfilling the will of God – is not following the Lord. It will not perfect the body. We will not come into the unity of the faith. We will not come into the perfect man. We will not come into the measure of the stature of the fullness of Christ. We will fail to come into our destiny - the image of Christ - and stay in our current state, measured by the image of a single man.

If Ball is god, if Babylon is god, follow it. If our programs, our ambitions, our buildings are god, follow it. If the Lord is God, follow Him. Whatever we worship is our God. Our programs, our buildings, our theology will become our gods and we will serve them. We will not follow God's will if it jeopardizes any of the things that have become gods to us. We will not invite an apostle or prophet to come to speak into our local fellowship for fear that he will speak against the structure we are building. We must seek to follow God's will and build the church into His body. Then, He is our God.

The first principle in equipping the body to do the work of ministry is that we must leave every worldly way to follow the Lord. The second principle is that we must prepare the sacrifice. God wants our sacrifice, our ministry to Him to be pure.

Prepare the sacrifice.

Paul tells us to *"present your bodies a living sacrifice, holy, acceptable to God, which is your reasonable service. And do not be conformed to this world, but be transformed by the renewing of your mind, that you may prove what is the good and acceptable and perfect will of God."* (Romans 12:1,2)

Paul tells us that we ought to be a holy sacrifice, acceptable to God. In the next sentence, he tells us how to do this. *"Do not be conformed to this world." "Come out of her my people,"* come out of our worldly ways. Paul wasn't talking to the unsaved, but the saved. In order for our sacrifice to be holy and acceptable - pure - to the Lord, we must not be conformed to the world, but we must come out of our worldly ways.

Depart from worldly ways in our ministry to God.

Our minds must be transformed from worldly minds to Kingdom minds. We must no longer think about ruling over people by intimidation and manipulation, but we must become servants, leading by inspiration.

But Jesus called them to Himself and said to them, "You know that those who are considered rulers over the Gentiles lord it over them, and their great ones exercise authority over them. Yet it shall not be so among you; but whoever desires to become great among you shall be your servant. And whoever of you desires to be first shall be slave of all. "For even the Son of Man did not come to be served, but to serve, and to give His life a ransom for many." (Mark 10:42-45)

If we are to do any ministry work, we cannot have an attitude of lording over God's people. God is the Lord of the people (the Head). The leader isn't the Head. I am not. You are not. If Jesus said he came to serve, not be served, how can anyone supposedly following Him desire to be served by those he is ministering to? If we do, we make ourselves the Lord, the God or the Head. Just because people have come into the position of having a servant's heart and desire to serve in the Kingdom doesn't mean they are to serve a man. They are to serve God in the way God has uniquely called them to serve. It is the leader's role to inspire them, to activate them, to give direction and oversight to those who want to serve God in order that their potential in God is maximized through their service to Him. They are not to be a leader's slave, but the leader is to be a servant to them. He serves them through accurate leadership, impartation, and inspiration.

It is the body's role to do the work of the ministry. It is not solely the leader's role to do the ministry work – that of spreading the word of God- it is the body's role. The leaders equip them to do it. They activate the gifts and callings of God in each saint's life.

Note that the will of God is not necessarily to promote the leader's ministry, but it is that God's will for each individual is done – that each individual comes into the image of Christ. If this is also the vision of the leader, then in following God's plan, his own ministry is also completed. It is only a selfish leader who seeks to promote his agenda over God's that will resist the direction of the Holy Spirit to serve the people. A selfish leader will enslave people to his ambitions. People in ministry realize what true ministry is - serving God's people. The higher ranking they achieve in the Kingdom, the more they will serve others. *"And whoever of you desires to be first shall be slave of all."* That's Jesus' plan for advancement in the Kingdom.

The first thing anyone who wants to do ministry work needs to realize is that we must not lord over people. Jesus said that is what the Gentiles do. That is a worldly structure. Jesus provides a greater example: that we must serve each other, *"For even the Son of Man did not come to be served, but to serve."*

The Old Testament gives us a good example of people who lord over others versus the model of the servant leader. Saul represents a leader who would lord over his people:

So Samuel told all the words of the LORD to the people who asked him for a king. And he said, "This will be the behavior of the king who will reign over you: He will take your sons and appoint them for his own chariots and to be his horsemen, and some will run before his chariots....
"He will take a tenth of your sheep. And you will be his servants."
(1Samuel 8:10-11, 17)

Saul represents a leader who will continually take from the people who serve him and will make them all his servants. God did not want a leader like that for Israel. But, because they insisted, he relented and allowed Saul to become king. Contrast this to the example set by David when he became king of Israel.

Then David danced before the LORD with all his might; and David was wearing a linen ephod. ... Then David offered burnt offerings and peace offerings before the LORD. And when David had finished offering burnt offerings and peace offerings, he blessed the people in the name of the LORD of hosts. Then he distributed among all the people, among the whole multitude of Israel, both the women and the men, to everyone a loaf of bread, a piece of meat, and a cake of raisins. (2 Samuel 6:14, 18,19)

David represented the kind of leader that Jesus calls us to be. Instead of commanding someone to dance in the celebration, he stripped off his kingly robes and led the procession, dancing before the Lord. He set the example of how the people ought to worship God. He inspired the people to worship God. Instead of commanding an offering from the people, he offered up a sacrifice to God. This set an example for all of Israel of how they ought to sacrifice to God. Instead of taking the best from the fields, the vineyards and the flocks of the Israelites, David gave of the best that he had. He gave meat to each family, instead of taking it from them. He gave bread for them to eat.

Anyone who wants to serve in ministry in the church needs to follow David's example. We need to give to the people. We don't look to the people to buy us something, to do something for us. We need to follow David's example and give something to the people we are ministering to. Jesus said we are to be loyal to the people we serve, not the other way around. If we always think of what we can get from others, instead of what we can give to others, we are acting like a gentile ruler.

No ministry in the church is greater than any other is. God is no respecter of persons. An usher is just as important as a teacher. The person who works the sound booth is as important as a pastor is. The only difference is that in one, we minister to people's physical needs and in the other to their spiritual needs. The pastor is there to equip and protect. The usher may actually do more ministering to people's needs than the pastor may. Each member is supposed to be out spreading the gospel. God wants us to become servants so that He may prove what the good and acceptable and perfect will of God is through us. This will happen when we come out of these worldly ways of looking for position, power, or control and are transformed into the character of Jesus and seek to serve by ministering to the people in our lives. The worldly structure is that men lord over men: that men are forced into the service of other men. The greatest in the worldly structure are those who are served by the most people. The Kingdom position is that we serve God by willingly serving each other. The greatest in the Kingdom are those who serve the most.

Our sacrifice must be of our own free will.

Let's look at some more principles by looking at how Israelites prepared the sacrifice. Read Leviticus 1:1-9

If his offering is a burnt sacrifice of the herd, let him offer a male without blemish; he shall offer it of his own free will at the door of the tabernacle of meeting before the LORD.
(Leviticus 1:3)

> **The greatest in the Kingdom are those who serve the most.**

The word free will is translated from the Hebrew *ratsown*, which means to delight in doing something, to find pleasure in doing something, to voluntarily do something. We can no longer manipulate people into coming to programs and doing things for the church. Everything we do must be of our own free will.

You also say, "Oh, what a weariness" And you sneer at it, says the LORD of hosts. And you bring the stolen, the lame, and the sick; thus you bring an offering! Should I accept this from your hand? Says the LORD. But cursed be the deceiver who has in his flock a male, and makes a vow, but sacrifices to the Lord what is blemished-- for I am a great King, says the LORD of hosts, And My name is to be feared among the nations. (Malachi 1:13-14)   (underlining added for emphasis)

Our sacrifice is not freely given when we say *"Oh, what a weariness!"* Whatever we do for God, we cannot do it out of compulsion, saying *"Oh, what a weariness!"* Everything we do must be from our own free will. We must find pleasure in doing the things we do for God. When we find ourselves weary in doing church work, we need to ask ourselves, "Am I serving God, or the church's programs?" The sacrifice done in weariness to serve the needs of the church may get us promoted in a worldly structure, but it doesn't earn a promotion in the Kingdom. God will not accept such a sacrifice from us. One characteristic of someone bearing the fruit of the Spirit is joy. We are not promised that in everything we do we will find earthly pleasure in it. But the joy of the Lord should be found in it – if we are truly doing it for God – and not to please man.

We cannot bring the stolen. Each one of us has a unique ministry in the body of Christ. I can't do what you are supposed to do and you cannot do what I'm supposed to do. We shouldn't try to walk in someone else's anointing. This is a stolen sacrifice. If we go out and buy the books and tapes and go to the seminars, this doesn't mean we are to try to preach the same message. We need to do what we've been called to do, teach what we've been sent to teach, minister to the people we see every day. Don't steal someone else's sacrifice by trying to duplicate what they are doing.

Jesus said to the Pharisee Nicodemus: *"We speak what We know and testify what We have seen."* (John 3:11) In order for us to offer a sacrifice of our own free will, it must first of all be our own. To avoid the sin of the Pharisees, we must stick to what we know, do what we have been called to do, and testify to what we have seen. If a child goes out in her mother's clothes, it is obvious to everyone that she is playing dress-up. How many children in the ministry go out with their father's clothes, their father's anointing, and preach their father's sermons? In the Spirit, they are just playing dress-up. There won't be any true power in it because they are operating out of a Pharisee position. *"Therefore behold, I am against the prophets,"* says *the LORD, "who steal My words every one from his neighbor.* (Jeremiah 23:30) Only when we walk in Jesus' character, *"We speak what We know and testify what We have seen,"* can we carry His authority. Anything less than that are stolen sacrifices. What will minister to the people we meet is our own testimony. We need to let people know how God is making a difference in our lives, not try to preach the sermon we heard on Sunday, or what we saw last night on TBN. Revelation 12:11 *says, "And they overcame him by the blood of the Lamb and by the word of their testimony, and they did not love their lives to the death."* (Emphasis added)

Our sacrifice, our ministry, must be unblemished.

What is blemished? We cannot offer the lame or the sick. Whatever we do with God, we must give it our best. The word sick is translated from the Hebrew *chalah*, which means to be weak, sick, or afflicted. God doesn't want us to offer up any weak, afflicted, or sick sacrifice. He wants our sacrifice to be strong. If we're going to do anything with God, we should pray and prepare ourselves so that God's will is done, not our own. Whatever we do, we must give our absolute best.

In order to avoid offering up a weak, afflicted, sick sacrifice, we must avoid the sin of the Pharisee who only does things to be seen. We must first prepare ourselves through prayer. We must seek out God first. We cannot just show up and expect God to accept that kind of sacrifice. Let's not be hypocrites: pray in private before we offer up any public service. This way, when we pray for someone, there will be power behind it. Pray powerful prayers based on belief that comes from spending time with God. Don't offer up any weak, sick prayers. This goes not only for praying, but whatever our spiritual sacrifice is.

Our Ministry must be purged of selfish ambition.

*... but he shall wash its entrails and its legs with water. And the priest shall burn all on the altar as a burnt sacrifice, an offering made by fire, a sweet aroma to the Lord. (*Leviticus 1: 9)

We must clean our own sacrifice, our ministry. If a priest had offered up a sacrifice without cleaning it, it would have been foul smelling, not a sweet aroma unto the Lord. When we do things in the church in order to get a position of power, out of selfish ambition, we are doing it to glorify ourselves, not God. We have to allow God to cleanse us of these worldly ways. We have to allow Him to clean out the selfish ambition – always looking to promote ourselves. We must get rid of envy, condemnation, and control, and seek to glorify God.

"And now, O priests, this commandment is for you. If you will not hear, and if you will not take it to heart, to give glory to My name," says the LORD of hosts, "I will send a curse upon you, and I will curse your blessings. Yes, I have cursed them already, because you do not take it to heart. Behold, I will rebuke your descendants and spread refuse on your faces, the refuse of your solemn feasts; and one will take you away with it." (Malachi 2:1-3)

If we don't take it to heart to give glory to His Name but seek our power, position, and our own glory, God says His curse will be upon us, our descendants rebuked, and refuse is on our faces. In some churches everything is based on power, position and selfish ambition. *"Come out of her my people."* If we are in one of these churches, we push three people out of the way to get to sing – we're up in front of all the people singing our hearts out, but nothing happens, God doesn't hear. We hit every note, and everyone applauds, but no one was healed, no one was delivered. Why? While we were up there, God looked down and saw refuse on our faces - the refuse of our solemn feast. It wasn't **His** feast. It was **our** feast. We got up to show what we could do, not what God could do. We touched people's emotions, but didn't reach beyond the veil to their spirit. We cooked the cow without cleaning it. That isn't a sweet aroma to God – it's foul smelling. God cannot bless what He's already cursed.

We must prepare by spending time with Him. We must abide in His Word. Only then can He accept our sacrifice. Only when they are done in the Name, in the character, and under the authority of Jesus can He accept them. God wants us to give glory to His name. In very simple terms if we are going to go out and represent Him, go out in

His name, we ought to make Him pleased with us. How do we please God? When we go out in His name, we express His character and do things under his authority. We cannot do anything outside of God's character and expect Him to be pleased with us. In everything we do we need to check our motives. Am I doing this with God, or to promote myself? Am I doing this to please a man or to please God? Once we've properly prepared the sacrifice, we can then go on to build the altar.

Rebuild the altar that had been broken down.

In 1 Kings 18, we see the story about how Elijah confronted the prophets of Baal and called the men of Israel back to minister to the Lord.

Then Elijah said to all the people, "Come near to me." So all the people came near to him. And he repaired the altar of the LORD that was broken down. And Elijah took twelve stones, according to the number of the tribes of the sons of Jacob, to whom the word of the LORD had come, saying, "Israel shall be your name." Then with the stones he built an altar in the name of the LORD. (I Kings 18:30-32)

Elijah didn't just throw the sacrifice on the ground and expect God to honor it. He took 12 stones and built the altar. The number 12 represents government. Just as Elijah rebuilt the altar of sacrifice, the modern day Elijah will build up the platform for our sacrifice, the church. What has been broken down in our altar – the church? Everything done in the church that is not in the character and under the authority – in the Name - of Jesus is broken down. *"Return, O backsliding children,"* says the LORD. (Jeremiah 3:14) How do we leave our backsliding state? *"And I will give you shepherds according to My heart, who will feed you with knowledge and understanding."* (Jeremiah 3:15)

The church today needs to embrace its shepherds, the five-fold ministry, to leave our backsliding state and come to Zion. The church today is broken down if it does not include the foundational ministries of apostles and prophets in its structure. So, just as Elijah laid 12 stones to form the foundation of the altar that had become broken down, Jesus will use the apostles and prophets to set the foundation for His church. Why is proper foundation important to the church? Without it, it would remain in a state of being broken down. It will continue to be unable to support the sacrifice it is supposed to bear. *"Then with the stones he built an altar in the name of the LORD."*

The sacrifice the church is supposed to produce is a body of people who have arrived at the fullness of the stature of Christ – a body of people that show forth His Glory to the world. So God is rebuilding the church with the proper structure so it can be equipped and transformed into the perfect man – the man who will be in His image and have His authority.

What does this have to do with the subject, the equipping the saints for the work of ministry? Paul told the church at Ephesus that the church was being built up into a dwelling place of the Lord. Just as in a building each stone must be supported by another, and all are supported by the foundation, in the church structure each living stone must be connected to another and supported by the foundational stones. Elijah didn't throw his sacrifice on ground. He put it on the altar that he rebuilt.

In the same way our sacrifice, whether it is individuals ministering in the marketplace or the work of a local fellowship, shouldn't be thrown out on the ground, but offered up on the altar. The altar is the Church. Each individual and ministry needs to be accountable and connected to someone else. Any individual or ministry that does not make itself accountable to someone else withdraws from the body.

Likewise you younger people, submit yourselves to your elders. Yes, all of you be submissive to one another, and be clothed with humility, for "God resists the proud, but gives grace to the humble." (1 Peter 5:5)

Obey those who rule over you, and be submissive, for they watch out for your souls, as those who must give account. Let them do so with joy and not with grief, for that would be unprofitable for you. (Hebrews 13:17)

The key to being equipped for the work of the ministry is submission. As we discussed earlier, it is not enslavement to someone else's ministerial ambitions. It is in submission to God's ordained structure that He edifies us and builds us up into His image. God does not desire for us to be enslaved, but he desires for us to be connected to the rest of the body so we can be transformed into the image of Christ. It is the responsibility of those to whom we submit ourselves to inspire us, to lead us, and to help connect us with our purpose in God.

Just as Elijah rebuilt the altar before offering up his sacrifice by building with 12 stones representing all of Israel, the church will include representation from every race. The reformed church is not going to be split along racial, cultural, or even denominational lines, but it is going to be knit together with each joint supplying, in order to grow into the stature of the fullness of Christ.

All practices in our ministry work that are not directly from God will be quenched.

The next thing Elijah did was pour water on the sacrifice that had been properly laid on the altar. This was done in order to insure that no artificial fires were kindled, but that any fire would have to come from God Himself. In the same way, God is going to pour out the water of His Word on His sacrifice, the Church. The word will go out to quench out all the man-inspired practices in the church. It will destroy all the worldly ways. It will expose our motives to rule over the people instead of serve them or our desire to intimidate instead of inspire. Any program we establish from our minds will not stand up to the Word of God. The Word of God will quench each one out.

Eliminating worldly ways from the church is part of the ministry of the five-fold. Just as Elijah used four waterpots, so God will not just use one vessel to pour out the word, but many. He will use apostles and prophets, evangelists, teachers and pastors. Each one will come with one pot full of water - one word from God. And just as Elijah said, "Do it again," many will come again and again, until what they have been sent to impart to this city, this nation, has been received. They will make adjustments to the local body. They will point out those things that are out of God's order. They will not do this through their own understanding. But, they will deliver to the local body the Word of God. They will act in the authority of the office in which God has established them.

Any ministry which will not submit itself to the pouring out of the water of the Word of God will not have the man-made fires quenched out. If we do not quench out all of the man-made fires, we cannot receive the fire that only comes from heaven. Bringing some hot coals into the altar was probably a trick that the Baal worshipers used to trick the people into thinking their god was bringing down fire. Elijah wanted them to understand that there was no trickery involved. He completely soaked the sacrifice to remove any possibility that there was some kind of hidden fire. The same way, we need to invite the same level of scrutiny into our ministry to ensure that there are not hidden man-made fires involved: no hidden agendas; no self promotion; no selfish ambition; no desire to build up our own kingdom. This is how the saints are equipped for ministry: they receive the word from a pastor. Then another – a prophet - comes and "does it again." Then another – an evangelist - "does it again." God keeps pouring out His word on us until "Christ is formed in us." (Galatians 4:19) Then, we can be sure that anything that happens will be the result of the fire of God coming into His people. It is only when our man-made ambitions are removed that God can trust us with His fire: the fire of the Holy Ghost, the fire of the creative God in which everything that we say will come to pass.

> **Once the fire of God has purified His Church, we will see the great revival – the harvest of souls - we have been waiting for.**

Purified by Fire

The next thing Elijah did was make a proclamation:

Lord God of Abraham, Isaac and Israel, let it be known this day that You are God in Israel and I am Your servant, and that I have done all these things at your word. Hear me O Lord, hear me, that this people may know that You are the Lord God, and that You have turned their hearts back to You again. (1 Kings 18: 36-37)

We need to proclaim the Word of God into the earth. This is the key to establishing the Kingdom of God in the earth. We need to declare the will of God. If we do everything else properly, but do not step into the governing position in God that He has established the church in, we will fail to establish His kingdom in the earth. He doesn't speak these things into the earth. He depends on a people to hear Him and declare these things to the people.

Elijah proclaimed that Israel would turn their hearts back to God. It was then that fire came down from heaven and consumed the sacrifice, the wood, the stones and the dust and the water. Then the people said: *"The Lord, He is God. The Lord, He is God."*

In the same way it will be when we allow the fire of God to consume us, to consume our churches, to consume our work, that people will no longer be able to see us, but when they look at us all they will see is the God in us. Then we are ready to release people into ministry work. They won't see churches fighting with one another; they will see the body of Christ. It is when the Church is built into the unity of the faith and we are built into the stature of the fullness of Christ that we will see this mighty move of God we have all been waiting for. It is when the unsaved can see Jesus in us that they will see that the Jesus we proclaim is truly God. Then they will say, "The Lord, He is God." They will say, "There is no way they could do this without God. There is no way they can love each other so purely without God. There is no way they can work miracles without God." They will say, *"The Lord, He is God."* This is the equipped worker God wants to release.

Once the fire of God has purified His Church, we will see the great revival – the harvest of souls - we have been waiting for. We will say as Isaiah said: *"Who are these who fly like a cloud, and like doves to their roosts? Surely the coastlands shall wait for Me; and the ships of Tarshish will come first, to bring your sons from afar, their silver and their gold with them, to the name of the LORD your God, and to the Holy One of Israel, because He has glorified you."* (Isaiah 60:8-9) This will happen when the Church is purified so it can carry the Glory of the Lord. Isaiah says they come to you because "He has glorified you." So it is only when we show God's glory that we can receive the fire of God - that fire of God to which people will be attracted.

What happens to those who will not submit themselves to God's authority on the earth? What happens to those who will not depart from worldly ways? What happens to those who do not prepare themselves? What happens to those who are not built into God's altar, the church? What happens to those who will not extinguish all ungodly practices? What happens to those who continue to sacrifice to Baal, in spite of the word of the Lord calling them to repentance?

And Elijah said to them, "Seize the prophets of Baal! Do not let one of them escape!" So they seized them; and Elijah brought them down to the Brook Kishon and executed them there. (I Kings 18:40)

Who did Elijah call on to kill the prophets of Baal? He called on those who had repented and come back to the Lord. So if the prophets of Baal had repented like the rest of Israel, they would have been spared. But it is often the leaders who have the most to lose who are the last to repent. The word brook where the prophets of Baal were killed is translated from the Hebrew: *nachal*: a stream, especially a winter torrent. The brook or torrent Kishon represents a place of God's deliverance from oppression. When the Caananite King Sisera came against Israel, he was defeated at the Brook Kishon. So the judgment of the prophets of Baal at the brook Kishon represents God's swift judgment against those opposed to Him. So should anyone who is practicing worldly principles and opposing the will of God fear the same swift judgment.

The Measure of the Stature
of the Fullness of Christ

Ephesians 4:13 *...till we all come to the unity of the faith and of the knowledge of the Son of God, to a perfect man, to the measure of the stature of the fullness of Christ;* (NKJV)

[That it might develop] until we all attain oneness in the faith and in the comprehension of the [full and accurate] knowledge of the Son of God, that [we might arrive] at really mature manhood (the completeness of personality which is nothing less than the standard height of Christ's own perfection), the measure of the stature of the fullness of the Christ and the completeness found in Him. (Amplified Bible)

In this chapter we will explore:
• The unity of the faith
• The knowledge of the Son of God
• A perfect man
• The measure of the stature of the fullness of Christ.

The Unity (oneness) of the Faith

The unity of the faith is oneness with the Father, through which we are one with each other. Jesus describes the unity (oneness) of the faith in His prayer for the Church.

"Now I am no longer in the world, but these are in the world, and I come to You. Holy Father, keep through Your name those whom You have given Me, that they may be one as We are... I do not pray for these alone, but also for those who will believe in Me through their word; that they all may be one, as You, Father, are in Me, and I in You; that they also may be one in Us, that the world may believe that You sent Me." (John 17:11, 20-21)

We need to be one with the Father in the same way as Jesus was. Jesus didn't do anything on His own. He only did what He saw the Father doing. So we need to be the same way. We need to constantly listen for what God is saying, what His will is, and do it. The more we seek Him, the more we study His word, the more we pray in the Spirit, the more we worship Him, the more we will become like Him and become one with Him. It is when we are one with the Father and the Son that the world will see Jesus in us and believe.

*And the glory which You gave Me I have given them, that they may be one just as We are one... (*John 17:22)

> **The unity of the faith is oneness with the Father, through which we are one with each other.**

When we receive the fullness of the Holy Spirit and the gifts of the Spirit, this is the first step to the glory of God being manifested in us. So receiving the gifts and the person of the Holy Spirit into our lives is essential to fulfilling the will of God for our lives: that we become one with Him.

*I in them, and You in Me; that they may be made perfect in one, and that the world may know that You have sent Me, and have loved them as You have loved Me. (*John 17:23)

Jesus says that we are to ***be made perfect in one,"*** or perfect in unity, by receiving Him into our lives. If we are to be one with Him, we must abide in Him. We must remain in Him. This only comes through prayer and revelation by which we see who Jesus is. The word has to become flesh and dwell in us. Just as Jesus became flesh and dwelt on earth, so He has to become part of our flesh and dwell in us. Jesus has to be in us - *"I in them"* - for us to *"be made perfect in one."* So, it is when we have received Jesus completely and made Him part of our life, our existence, when we as a Church have become perfect in one - or perfect in unity - that the world will know that God sent Him. This is part of the great end-time harvest. People will see the glory of God on the unified Church and come in.

The unity of the faith is not that we are to try to force everyone into believing the same thing. But, the unity of the faith is that we become one with the Father and the Son by receiving the person and glory of Jesus. It is when we corporately are one with the Father and the Son that we will be able to see each other as He sees us. Then we will be able to be one (in unity) with each other. Then, we can love each other as He loves us. When we are one with Him, then we can be one with each other and come into the oneness (unity) of the faith.

The Knowledge of the Son of God

"Father, I desire that they also whom You gave Me may be with Me where I am, that they may behold My glory which You have given Me; for You loved Me before the foundation of the world." (John 17:24)

Jesus said He desired that we be with Him where He was. He is talking about an intimate relationship with Him where we truly know Him in every aspect. We know His love. We know His heart. We understand His will. Just as Jesus did this while He was on earth, we can too. This is essential to our being one with Him: while we are on earth, we need to be in an intimate relationship with God. When we come into this relationship, we will be able to behold His glory, the glory He had before the foundations of the world.

This is what is meant by *the knowledge of the Son of God"* in Ephesians 4:13: we are to have an intimate relationship with Him. He also says that we are to know Him in His glory. All of the apostles had an intimate relationship with Him and saw Jesus' goodness and loving character. But not all the disciples saw him in his splendor before his death and resurrection. Peter, James, and John were able to see His glory manifested on earth when Christ was transfigured before them on the mount. What was required before they saw Jesus in His glory?

Now it came to pass, about eight days after these sayings, that He took Peter, John, and James and went up on the mountain to pray. And as He prayed, the appearance of His face was altered, and His robe became white and glistening. (Luke 9:28-29)

The key to knowing Him in His glory is prayer. We won't just stumble upon Him in His glory. We will find Him in His glory through prayer. Peter, James, and John went up on the mountain to pray. That is where they saw Jesus in His glory. Did the rest of disciples see Jesus in His glory? No. They were down in the city fighting a demon. Not only did the other disciples miss seeing Jesus in His glory because they didn't go to pray, but they couldn't walk in His authority at this time. Why? It was because of lack of prayer.

He *answered and said, "O faithless generation, how long shall I be with you? How long shall I bear with you? Bring him to me."* (Mark 9: 19)

And He said unto them, "This kind can come out by nothing but by prayer and fasting." (Mark 9:29)

What Jesus was telling His disciples was that they were a *"faithless generation,"* or faithless group of people. He said, *"how long shall I bear with you."* He said that he was tiring of trying to teach them something. They did not have faith enough to do it. When they asked Him why they couldn't cast out the demon, Jesus told them this kind will not come out without prayer and fasting. He said he couldn't release them into the kind of ministry that they would walk in His anointing until they learned to pray and fast. Jesus took Peter, James, and John up on the mountain to pray. They beheld His glory. But the other nine stayed in town and then they questioned, "Why could we not cast it out?" Jesus was telling them, you should have come up on the mountain with us to pray and fast, to see me in My glory, to truly know Me, then you could come forth with power, with faith filled power.

We should not be like the nine disciples who had no power in this situation. But there is good news: even eight of the nine who had trouble with the demon in this story eventually learned to pray and fast and gain authority over the enemy. These same were filled with the Holy Spirit on the day of Pentecost and spread the Gospel to the nations. If they initially failed but eventually succeeded, then so can we – if we also learn to pray and fast to get to know Him better.

> **The key to seeing the glory of Jesus is prayer and fasting.**

A Perfect Man

The word perfect comes from the Greek *teleios*: complete (in various applications of labor, growth, mental and moral character), completeness: of full age, man, perfect. Some interpret this scripture to mean that we are to become really mature Christians. Rich Elliot defines perfection as perfect worship of God. (Rich Elliot, Daily Milk and Honey, e-mail publication, River of Revival Ministries, Lawrence, Kansas)

When I read this scripture I spent considerable time studying the phrase, "the perfect man." What does it mean? Does it mean that the purpose of the church is to produce perfect people? Does it mean that each of us will reach this state of perfection - "until we all come to the unity of the faith, the knowledge of the Son of God, the perfect man" – before Jesus returns? Does it mean to "become mature" as the New International Version translates it? This is an important verse because it points out the primary goal of the church, so it is important in everything we do to understand what Paul was saying here as we go to build this church. We have to understand the blueprints, the Word of God.

As I was contemplating this and praying for God to show me the deeper meaning, he showed me a picture of a mosaic. A mosaic is a surface decoration made by inlaying small pieces of variously colored stones to form a picture or a decoration. This type of decoration was quite popular during the Roman times where they cemented stones together to form a decoration on a floor of a building or in a courtyard. This process makes very beautiful pictures. But, if you look quite closely, you can see that the individual stones that make up the mosaic are all imperfect. They have various imperfections, rough spots, jagged edges, and small discolorations. But when pieced together, they form a beautiful picture. This is what God was trying to show me.

He is building a beautiful mosaic called the body of Christ. This body, when it is finished, will be the "perfect man." As he says in Ephesians 5:27, He will "present her to Himself a glorious church, not having spot or wrinkle or any such thing, but that she should be holy and without blemish." This church as a whole will be perfect. It will be without spot, wrinkle, or any such thing. It will be holy and without blemish. It will be a perfect picture of Christ, a mosaic where each of the members of the Body of Christ forms part of the whole perfect picture. If we look closely at each member, they may still have a few imperfections, but when you draw back to God's perspective, you will see how they form this perfect picture. From a distance you cannot see any imperfections (or you see them covered by the blood of Jesus). You just see a beautiful picture. How can we as a body reach this perfect man while on earth? By abiding in Christ, we can come into perfect union with Him through worship and prayer.

"I in them, and You in Me; that they may be made perfect in one, and that the world may know that You have sent Me, and have loved them as You have loved Me". (John 17:23)

It is coming into the same unity of the faith, being one with God, which perfects us. Jesus says that if He is in us, then we may be made perfect in one (unity). This is the completeness, maturity, which Jesus was speaking to and what he sent the five-fold ministry to produce.

"that they all may be one, as You, Father, are in Me, and I in You; that they also may be one in Us, that the world may believe that You sent Me." (John 17: 21)

This scripture clearly shows that we should desire the same perfect union with the Father as Jesus did. Otherwise how can we be one in Them? There is no sin in Them. Therefore, there should be no sin in us. There must be an intimacy with the Father and the Son, Christ in us, that overcomes the world. Some argue that we will come into this perfect unity in heaven. But these scriptures clearly demonstrate that we are to come into this intimacy with Them while on earth "that the world may believe that You sent Me." For the world to see us in union with the Father and the Son, we would have to be in the world – the world cannot see us if we were in heaven, because the world doesn't have access to heaven. So, we are to be one with the Father and the Son. Then, we can demonstrate God's love to the world.

Some may say, "this doesn't include me – I can never be perfected." Paul said: *"Him we preach, warning every man and teaching every man in all wisdom, that we may present every man perfect in Christ Jesus."* (Colossians 1:28) Again, the scripture is very

> **If we want to reveal Christ to the world, we need to be pure just as He is pure. Holiness to the Lord!**

clear: every man is to be presented perfect. How? We are perfect in Christ Jesus – from coming into unity with Him – from coming into intimate knowledge of Him. This is for everyone, not some religious elite. Just as salvation is not through us, but because of Jesus' sacrifice on the cross, this intimacy with the Father and the Son is not due to our own works, but again through Jesus.

Behold what manner of love the Father has bestowed on us, that we should be called children of God! Therefore the world does not know us, because it did not know Him. Beloved, now we are children of God; and it has not yet been revealed what we shall be, but we know that when He is revealed, we shall be like Him, for we shall see Him as He is.   And everyone who has this hope in Him purifies himself, just as He is pure.   (I John 3:1-3)

John says when Christ is revealed we shall be like Him and see Him as He is. If we want Christ to be revealed, if we want Christ to return, we must be like Him, and we must see Him as He is. We must have knowledge of Him, clear discernment of Him. We must desire to be with Him and see Him as He is. It is when His love is in us that we will reveal Him to the world because we see Him as He is – in His glory. John tells us how to do this. We need to purify ourselves just as He is pure. He doesn't hold up any great man like Moses, David, Abraham, or John the Baptist and say we should purify ourselves as they did. He told us to purify ourselves, as Christ Himself is pure. If we want to reveal Christ to the world, we need to be pure just as He is pure. Holiness to the Lord!

But whoever keeps His word, truly the love of God is perfected in him. By this we know that we are in Him. (1 John 2:5)

John tells us that we must keep His word to show the perfect love of God.   The word **keeps** is translated from the Greek *tereo* which means: to guard, to keep an eye on, to prevent from escaping, it implies a fortress or full military lines of apparatus, to note (a prophecy, to fulfill a command), to detain (in custody; to maintain) to hold fast, to keep. John says we ought to guard His word. We ought to post a military style encampment around His word. We ought to keep it in custody and do not let it escape. Why is His word so important? It is important because the enemy is always trying to get us to agree with his word instead of the word of God. To paraphrase, if you can quit agreeing with the accuser and start confessing, start putting a guard on, start protecting what comes out of your mouth, such that nothing escapes from it except the word of God, then we know that God's love is perfected in us. This is clear evidence that we are in an intimate relationship with Him.

Love has been perfected among us in this: that we may have boldness in the day of judgment; because as He is, so are we in this world.

There is no fear in love; but perfect love casts out fear, because fear involves torment. But he who fears has not been made perfect in love. (I John 4:17-18)

John says that when love is perfected in us (the church) we will be in the world as God is in heaven. Whatever God is doing in heaven, we do on earth – just like Him. Notice that John says we will be just like Him *"**in this world**."* We don't have to wait until we get to heaven to be perfected – we are to be perfected in this world. When love is perfect in us, we will be like Him in this world, not only when we get to heaven.

Charles Capps, in his book <u>The Tongue – a Creative Force</u>, defines **fear** as **"faith in the enemy's ability."** John says, *"perfect love casts out fear,"* and *"But he who fears has not been made perfect in love."* If we are perfect in love, then we will have faith in God. When we get faith in God, we no longer fear the enemy. So to be perfect in God, we have to get our faith in the right person. Abide in Jesus and let Him abide in you. Abide in the Word of God. Then you will have faith. *Faith comes by hearing and hearing by the word of God.* So, when we get His words in our mouth, when we get His word in our heart, then fear can no longer exist. Fear and faith in God cannot exist together. **We either have faith in God or faith in the enemy** (which is fear). When we get God's love in us we overcome fear. When we get God's love in us, we get God in us. Then we overcome the world.

God wants His Church to be in perfect worship of Him, perfect holiness to the Lord, perfect relationship with Him, while on earth. Ephesians 4:11-13 says that we'll stay right here getting perfected by apostles, prophets, evangelists and pastors and teachers until we become the perfect man. There will be no transformation of an imperfect church. Paul says in Ephesians 5:27 that He is coming back for *a "glorious church, not having spot, or wrinkle or any such thing, but that she should be holy and without blemish."* That is **the perfect man**. This is the perfect, fully developed, fully mature, completely holy and pure church that apostles, prophets, evangelists, and pastors and teachers are given to produce.

The measure of the stature of the fullness of Christ

For this reason I bow my knees to the Father of our Lord Jesus Christ, from whom the whole family in heaven and earth is named, that He would grant you, according to the riches of His glory, to be strengthened with might through His Spirit in the inner man, that Christ may dwell in your hearts through faith; that you, being rooted and grounded in love, may be able to comprehend with all the saints what is the width and length and depth and height-- to know the love of Christ which passes knowledge; that you may be filled with all the fullness of God. (Ephesians 3:14-19)

The measure of the stature of the fullness of God is Christ's fullness embodied in His church. Paul said the church was His fullness. (Ephesians 1:22-23) This is a people in unity with each other through being in unity with God. This is a church full of people who have seen the Glory of God manifested in their lives. This is a church full of people who through their unity with the Father demonstrate the love of God to the world. This is a church to which multitudes of people will flock to be saved because the church has been glorified. (Isaiah 60) The glory of the Lord is upon them. This church has been evaluated – measured – in every facet of the ministry, in every area of their lives, and was built correctly in every area. This church manifests Christ to the world - that the world may know that the Father sent Him.

I want to be part of building that church. How do we arrive there? By being strengthened by the Holy Spirit, *"that He would grant you, according to the riches of His glory, to be strengthened with might through His Spirit in the inner man."* We must allow Christ to dwell in our hearts through faith without fear. **We have to be rooted and grounded in love.** Then we can comprehend, take hold of, not just to know in our heads, but to grab, embrace, thoroughly realize the measure of Christ: the width, length, depth, and height of His love for us. Paul notes here that **this passes knowledge.** He isn't talking about fulfilling the letter of the law. He isn't talking about understanding the Bible and knowing all the books and memorizing scripture. Paul is talking about an intimate relationship with God that surpasses knowledge: anything in the soul or the flesh. It's not just understanding in the mind, willing to serve God or having great joy. This goes to intimate contact: we must know Him. We must embrace Him. We must embody Him individually and as His church. This is the measure of the stature of the fullness of Christ.

5

Freeing the Captives

Ephesians 4: 14   *...that we should no longer be children, tossed to and fro and carried about with every wind of doctrine, by the trickery of men, in the cunning craftiness of deceitful plotting...*

To paraphrase: it is the job of the five-fold ministry, the apostles, prophets, evangelists, pastors, and teachers, to teach sound doctrine and build up the body so they would not be deceived by those who by trickery and cunning craftiness of deceitful plotting are keeping the body of Christ as children. Once they are freed from this captivity they can be perfected and edified to become the fully mature, perfect man, even Christ operating in His body.

The word children is translated from the Greek: *nepios* (nay'-pee-os); not speaking, i.e. an infant (minor); figuratively, a simple-minded person, an immature Christian. A child, in this context, is a Christian who is unable to speak the Word of God and remains simple-minded and immature in Christ.

> **As long as we are kept as children, unable to speak the Word of God, then we can be kept as his slaves.**

Paul said that we would be kept as children, simple-minded, unable to speak, by the trickery of men. So men would trick us into being simple-minded, unable to speak the Word of God. Why would these men in the **cunning, craftiness of deceitful plotting** want to keep us ignorant by giving us **every wind of doctrine**? Why would they twist the Word in "**every wind of doctrine**" to manipulate, intimidate, and control the people of God and keep them unable to grow into the image of Christ? This is not necessarily the men, but the enemy using the men. The enemy does not want the church to come into the measure of the stature of Christ, so he unleashes every trick he has to stop us. Paul called this cunning craftiness. The enemy is using cunning craftiness and deceitful plotting to keep the people as babes, to control them, to keep them out of their ministry work. God wants them free. The enemy wants them kept in bondage to him. If he can keep them as children, then he will be able to control them, manipulate them and intimidate them into serving him in his programs instead of serving God.

What is the spirit that takes people captive?

What is the spirit that would allow men, even ministers of the Gospel, to be used by the enemy in this way? Jack Frost, in his teaching series, *From Slavery to Son-ship*, called this an orphan spirit. Men who haven't come into a relationship with the Father as a son can have an orphan spirit. An orphan operates as a slave instead of as a son. He doesn't know the guarantee of an inheritance, so he is always trying to gain approval. He is trying to perform, even in doing ministry work. He thinks if his ministry is bigger it will gain God's approval. So he does everything he knows to grow his ministry to gain God's approval, as well as the approval of his peers in the ministry. Paul called this position as bondage.

For ye have not received the spirit of bondage again to fear; but ye have received the Spirit of adoption, whereby we cry, Abba, Father. (Romans 8:15 KJV)

But the Father wants us to be sons crying *"Abba, Father"* instead of this bondage that forces us to perform out of a spirit of fear. Until we come into son-ship, we will be under bondage. But there is good news, *"There is therefore now no condemnation to them who are in Christ Jesus, who walk not after the flesh, but after the Spirit."* (Romans 8:1)

This is not a message of condemnation. If you have operated in this sprit of fear leading to bondage, you can come into adoption as a son, if you walk in the Spirit and not in the flesh. *"For as many as are led by the Spirit of God, they are the sons of God."* (Romans 8:14) This is what the Father wants. He wants you to come to him as a son crying "Abba, Father." He doesn't want us to perform and achieve according to works of the flesh (even in doing ministry work). But, instead he wants us to look to Him and do what He is doing. If He is saying "rest," then rest. If he is saying " work," then work. Jesus did whatever He saw the Father doing. If we are to be sons, we should do the same. So, the key to freeing those in captivity is to lead them out of bondage and into son-ship, by which they can call out to their Father, "Abba, Father." They can rest in the knowledge that whatever they do, they are still sons.

This is the lesson of the "prodigal" son found in Luke 15:11-32. Even though the son had done everything to earn his father's wrath, wasting all of his inheritance, the father still welcomes him back as son. It didn't matter that the "good" son had stayed with him and done everything he asked, the prodigal son still had the same position with the father – even though he had wasted everything on prostitutes and drinking. It's not our performance that God is after – it's our hearts. Once the son came back to the father with a heart of repentance and humility, he was welcomed back as a son. The son was willing to come back as a servant, but the father put on the ring that gave him authority to conduct business on his father's behalf – even though he had just wasted all of his inheritance. If we do the same and come to the Father with a heart of humility and repentance, how much more will he put His authority into us as His sons? *"For as many as are led by the Spirit of God, they are the sons of God."*

And if you are Christ's, then you are Abraham's seed, and heirs according to the promise. Now I say that the heir, as long as he is a child, does not differ at all from a slave, though he is master of all. (Galatians 3:29-4:1)

Paul said that if I am a child (the same Greek word *nepios*), then I am the same as a slave. We will be slaves to the cunning craftiness of men, who use weapons of control and intimidation to keep us captive. I am the **master of all**, but the enemy would have me believe I am a slave through the trickery of men. As long as we are kept as children, unable to speak the Word of God, then we can be kept as his slaves. But our Father wants us to move from being a slave, from being a child, into son-ship in which we are masters of all.

And because you are sons, God has sent forth the Spirit of His Son into your hearts, crying out "Abba Father!" Therefore you are no longer a slave but a son, and if a son, then an heir of God through Christ. (Galatians 4:6-7)

It is through becoming sons of the Father that we are freed from the slavery of sin. We are no longer slaves. So, to free the captives, we need to introduce them to the love of the Father through which we became heirs of God. We need to understand that we are masters of all. We are no longer slaves to men or slaves to sin. We are heirs of God himself. This makes us masters of all.

My little children, for whom I labor in birth again until Christ is formed in you, (Galatians 4:19)

In this verse, Paul referred to the Galatians as little children: *teknon.* They were not referred to as the infants, *nepios*, unable to speak, but as little children. He said he was trying to form Christ in them. He was trying to free them from the captivity of the traditions that were trying to enslave them and form Christ in them. This is what Paul says the five-fold ministry was given to do: to free the captives from enslavement to traditions, from enslavement to trickery of men, from enslavement of deceitful plotting and form Christ in the people.

Tell me, you who desire to be under the law, do you not hear the law? For it is written that Abraham had two sons: the one by a bondwoman, the other by a freewoman. But he who was of the bondwoman was born according to the flesh, and he of the freewoman through promise, which things are symbolic. For these are the two covenants: the one from Mount Sinai which gives birth to bondage, which is Hagar-- for this Hagar is Mount Sinai in Arabia, and corresponds to Jerusalem which now is, and is in bondage with her children--but the Jerusalem above is free, which is the mother of us all. (Galatians 4:21-26)

Anything done in the flesh will result in bondage. Hagar represents that which is done in the flesh. She represents the ministry that goes forth before its time, operating in the flesh out of an orphan spirit, always trying to do something to gain the Father's love. She represents ministry that tries to produce out of the sweat of the brow, not doing what the Father is doing. She represents the old order.

In the new covenant, the promise of Abraham was transferred to Jesus' seed – the Church. This New Jerusalem is free. Paul wants us to be free of the bondage that comes through trying to do things in the flesh. If we are fulfilling the ministry we dream up or the one we have read about in the most popular how-to books on building a ministry, not necessarily that which God has willed for us, but something that will make us look good to our peers, then we are doing things in the flesh, not in the Spirit. In the process, we will enslave people to us to fulfill our idea of the ministry.

But we have been called out of bondage from things of the flesh and into the New Jerusalem, the Church. This is the son of promise, the promise of the Spirit. This Church operates on God's timing doing God's will. It doesn't do things that are politically motivated to gain approval. The New Jerusalem church doesn't try to build something that will look respectable or bring in lots of money. It only does the will of the Father. In this environment there will be freedom. Christ is the head of this ministry, not a man. When man is the head of the ministry he will do things to promote the ministry he has in mind – out of selfish ambition. When the ministry is submitted to doing the will of God, and Christ is the head of the ministry, we will operate in the Spirit.

Beware lest anyone cheat you through philosophy and empty deceit, according to the tradition of men, according to the basic principles of the world, and not according to Christ. (Colossians 2:8)

We must beware when someone starts teaching philosophy according to the principles of the world, not by the Word of God. These things of the world appear right, but they are really a delusion, empty deceit. To the carnal, they will sound right, but they are spiritually void. The ministry that is walking according to the flesh will turn to these programs to keep them active, make it look like they are going somewhere. But these things will not lead to freedom, but to bondage.

Let no one cheat you of your reward, taking delight in false humility and worship of angels, intruding into those things which he has not seen, vainly puffed up by his fleshly mind, and not holding fast to the Head, from whom all the body, nourished and knit together by joints and ligaments, grows with the increase that is from God. (Colossians 2:18-19)

Paul says not to let anyone cheat us of the reward the Father has for us when we enter the kingdom. There will be people who try to cheat us out of our reward. Paul again warns us to beware of them. They will teach doctrines of false humility. This is secular humanism: trying to obtain in

> **Every joint, every ligament, every member of the body has a part in ministering to you, perfecting you.**

the flesh what can only be truly obtained in the Spirit. The fleshly man cannot discern that which is Spirit, so when he talks about them, he *intrudes into those things which he has not seen.* He uses his puffed-up, fleshly mind to try to expound on these things. These things done in the flesh will never result in spiritual growth. So, we will be robbed of our reward if we follow the fleshly route. Since the carnal man cannot access the Father by the Spirit, he becomes the head of the church. He, in his puffed-up mind, takes on Christ's role as Head of the church.

But instead of adhering to fleshly principles, we are *to grow with the increase that is from God.* We will *be nourished and knit together by the joints and ligaments.* Notice that there is not one source of nourishment – not a fleshly head, but joints and ligaments. Every joint, every ligament, every member of the body has a part in ministering to you, perfecting you. This is not a one-man show. The body has to be knit together by the joints and ligaments. Some false head does not hold it together from above. The only way a controller can hold it together is in the flesh – which results in bondage. Instead, God uses every joint, every ligament, to nourish you.

This is not to say that there shouldn't be divine order in the body. Hebrews 13:17 tells us to *"Obey those who rule over you, and be submissive, for they watch out for your souls, as those who must give account. Let them do so with joy and not with grief, for that would be unprofitable for you."* Elders in a local assembly are given the responsibility to ensure that you are fed the word of God and built up into the head, which is Christ. They are not to be the head, but they are to watch out for your souls. Note that God's plan is to have more than one minister in the local assembly. The scripture says obey **"those,"** not obey "him." Having plurality of leadership will keep us from becoming dependent on and idolizing one man. Idolizing a man will rob you of your reward and will not perfect you, but put you into bondage. Submitting to righteous leadership, on the other hand, will allow you to be molded and perfected into the saint God wants you to be. Submitting to Godly leadership will put you into connection with the rest of the body of Christ that can supply you through the joints and ligaments and will also allow you to supply that which you are uniquely qualified to supply to the Body.

How do you discern the spirit that takes people captive? There is a spirit that keeps people as children, unable to learn, unable to speak the Word of God, unable to know God. So, it is critical to freeing those in captivity, marching in the wrong camp, to understand this spirit of fear that is behind those who manipulate and control them. If any minister has fallen into any of these traps, we need to repent quickly and ask God's forgiveness and forgiveness of those we have offended. But what are the traps we need to avoid if we are to lead people to liberty instead of captivity? Paul warned Timothy about these traps in his second letter to Timothy:

But know this, that in the last days perilous times will come: For men will be lovers of themselves, lovers of money, boasters, proud, blasphemers, disobedient to parents, unthankful, unholy... (2 Timothy 3:1-2)

The men who lead people into captivity are "lovers of themselves." When we minister, we cannot be selfish. We cannot promote our own interests instead of preparing the body to do the work of the ministry. We cannot put ourselves first so we look good, instead of preparing others for ministry. This isn't ministry to God. It is self-promotion.

We shouldn't be "lovers of money." If we are covetous, we will use deceitful, cunning tricks to separate people from their money. It may be a sad story or it may be as bold as demanding money to get a prophetic word, or as audacious as threatening to blackball someone if they do not support us. Whatever manipulation is used to separate people from their money, it is not from God if it is based on covetousness of the minister.

We cannot be boasters. Remember that the enemy will use all sorts of trickery and deceit to keep the people of God as children, unable to speak. One of these cunning plots is to keep people looking towards men instead of God. A boaster will speak of the things he has done. He will talk about the demons **he** has cast out. He will speak of the miracles **he** has performed. He draws attention **to himself**, instead of drawing people to God. This keeps the attention focused on the boaster and is meant to make the boaster seem irreplaceable: "If this person is so great, we better let him perform."

The subtle statement is that others would never be able to do it as well as the boaster. This deceit keeps the body of Christ from functioning properly. It keeps every joint from supplying. Instead, the boaster remains at the center of attention while others are held back from advancing to their potential in Christ where they can supply to the body what they were supposed to give.

We cannot be proud. The word translated proud is the Greek *huperephanos*; which means appearing above others (conspicuous), haughty. When we are proud, we have a great need to be the one in front, always seen, appearing above others. We have great pride in ourselves and contempt for others. This attitude of pride causes us to think we have to do everything ourselves. If we are caught up in pride we think we are the ones who were appointed for the task, so we start believing we should do everything, since only we could do it right. As a result, the body is idle so that we can demonstrate our anointing.

We cannot be <u>blasphemous</u>. We cannot hold ourselves in such high esteem that we do not fear even railing against God. Once pride takes over we can get so bold as to declare that we are Head of the local church – taking on Christ's title. But Christ told the apostles, *"But you be not called Rabbi: for one is your Teacher, even Christ; and all you are brothers."* (Matthew 23:8 KJV) Jesus made it very clear that Christ was the Teacher and they were all "brothers."

> **The men who take you captive will be lovers of themselves, lovers of money, boasters, proud, blasphemers, disobedient to parents, unthankful, and unholy.**

We cannot be <u>disobedient to parents</u>. If we are to serve God, we need to honor our parents. Some of us have issues with how we were raised. Some of us did not get the love we needed from our parents. We need to forgive them and reconcile with them. If we cannot honor the father and mother God gave us, then how do we honor God?

We cannot be <u>unthankful</u>. We cannot see it as people's duty to serve our ministry and us. If we do, we will be ungrateful for anything anyone does for us or gives us. We will start thinking we deserve it for being so great! If we are unthankful, we will use people, always trying to get more out of the people who serve us, never giving anything back or showing any true thanks, except in such degree as to manipulate people into giving even more.

We cannot be <u>unholy</u>, without consecration to God. If we are stuck in the flesh, we cannot worship God or submit to God to receive His purity – which is holiness. Lacking confidence in the Father's love, we will try even harder to appear holy before the people, putting on a show in prayer, always taking the lead in any form of worship, never giving anyone else a chance to contribute to the body. We start to fear that anyone else would come forward and appear holier than we do. So we keep the people as children, unable to speak, so we can appear to be the holy ones.

...unloving, unforgiving, slanderers, without self-control, brutal, despisers of good... (2 Timothy 3:3)

We cannot be <u>unloving</u>. One has to receive the Father's love to give it out. If we aren't full of the Father's love we get consumed with our agenda and ourselves. We will be hard hearted towards others. Without the Father's love, we only look to take, so we never even think to give back love. We will start to think it is the people's job to love us, because we are the anointed one. Without the Father's love, loving others would open us up to getting hurt, and we are too selfish to do anything that might cause any pain in our own lives.

> **The men who take you captive will be unloving, unforgiving, slanderers, without self-control, brutal, and despisers of good.**

We cannot be <u>unforgiving.</u> This word comes from the Greek *aspondos:* without libation (which usually accompanied a treaty). The King James Version translates this word as truce-breakers. Men that take people captive, operating in the flesh, will pursue their own agenda. They have no concept of God's principle of covenant relationship between man and God or between men. They think that covenant means the people commit to serving them in the same way they are trying to gain the Father's approval by serving him – not a mutual relationship between the two out of love and acceptance.

If we operate in the flesh, we will not forgive anyone whom we perceive as having wronged us. We will not tolerate anyone challenging our authority. We will not forgive that. We will not show any loyalty to others, especially those who serve us. We will not honor the level of relationship that we demand from those serving us, but we will betray the trust that is placed in us by the people. If we operate in the flesh, we are truce-breakers. We will break the covenants between men as we break God's covenant with them as shepherds. If we are to be true ministers we have to forgive, we have to honor relationships.

A trait of men that take people captive is that they are slanderers. This word is translated from the Greek *diabolos*. If we are operating in the flesh, in cunning craftiness that comes from the accuser of the brethren, we will lie to the people to keep them in submission to us. We will not hesitate to dress down and humiliate one of the children in order to solidify our control over the rest. We will spread lies about others to make us appear to be the only ones who are holy. If we are operating in the flesh, we will never speak truthfully to the people and let them know who they are in Christ. We will slander the people by calling them sinners, even those whom Christ has purified by His blood. We will use these lies to keep the people feeling unworthy to do anything in the body of Christ, so they will have to look up to us to do everything for them, the unworthy ones. So we take the place of *el Diablo*, accusing the people of sin, damning them, in order to elevate ourselves in their sight.

We cannot be without self-control or brutal. Without the love of the Father, we will fiercely attack the people for their faults, or for any transgression against us. We will not build up the people to understand who they are in Christ, but we will tear them down for failing to serve us in the capacity we are accustomed to. These attacks will inflict significant damage to the individual suffering under it. This opens up the individuals to demonic attacks of condemnation. They then are held in captivity by demonic forces of fear. Instead, we need to exhibit the fruit of the Spirit – love and self-control.

We cannot <u>despise those that are good</u>. If we lack true understanding of who God is we will despise the true virtue of God manifested in true worshipers. The carnal will mistake humility and meekness for weakness. Those who take people captive will assault the meek so they look foolish in the eyes of others. Then, they will not portray the same traits. This keeps us appearing to be on the moral high ground. It is a self-sustaining process. We lack the true relationship with the Father, so we will attack anyone who displays it. We feel threatened by the anointed ones so we attack them to hold on to our position in the church.

traitors, headstrong, haughty, lovers of pleasure rather than lovers of God... (2 Timothy 3:4)

We cannot be <u>traitors</u>. We cannot betray trust in order to increase our influence or take credit for the work of anointed individuals in order to appear to be anointed ourselves.

And from such people turn away! (2 Timothy 3:5)

We cannot be <u>headstrong.</u> The Greek word literally means falling forward. In other words, their heads are so big they risk falling on their faces. *Pride goes before destruction and a haughty spirit before a fall.* (Proverbs 16:18) This is a picture of this word. When we are caught up in pride, we fall over face first.

Men who take people captive are <u>haughty</u>, which is translated from the Greek: *tuphoo,* which means to envelop with smoke, i.e. (figuratively) to inflate with self-conceit. If we are in the flesh, trying to gain the Father's approval, we can get so caught up in the cloud of ourselves we cannot see accurately the state of our own souls. Because we see ourselves in such high regard, we never look to others to supply anything in the local church. We have to do everything. Nobody could ever do it as well as we could. We believe we are indispensable. So we cannot see other people as anything but speechless children. We would never consider that other people would be the one with the key ingredient in the local church. We cannot conceive that anyone else could contribute anything significant.

When we operate in the flesh, we are <u>lovers of pleasure more than (they are) lovers of God</u>. We are more concerned with our own physical desires than we are fulfilling the purposes of God. So we will always take the course that benefits us the most - that satisfies our desires - instead of the tougher course that will fulfill the will of God.

...having a form of godliness but denying its power. And from such people turn away! (2 Timothy 3:5)

When we operate in the flesh, we may <u>have a form of godliness but deny its power</u>. Many people act religious. This is the form of godliness. Many people think that spiritual gifts are a form of godliness. We may think that gifts validate a person's ministry. It is important to remember that the enemy can imitate genuine miracles. If we mistake the forms like acting religious or manifesting some signs for true godliness and follow those people, these same people may take us captive.

For of this sort are those who creep into households and make captives of gullible women loaded down with sins, led away by various lusts... (2 Timothy 3:6)

What was the reason Paul gave for telling Timothy to turn away from this sort of person? The first thing he says they do is creep into households. They sneak around in cunning craftiness and with deceitful plotting. They then take their victims **captive**. How do they take us captive? We are led away by various lusts. Note that it says **various** lusts. We are led away by our lust to be prophesied to instead of hearing God for ourselves. We are led away by our lust to part of a big ministry with a nice building. We are led away by our lust to have a position in the ministry that he is offering us if we will serve him. We are led into bondage of captivity.

True ministers will lead people into freedom, which is Christ. These men make them captive to themselves. Who is he able to take captive? He is not taking captive mature, perfected saints, but silly, gullible women. I don't think this is reserved only to females, but anyone who is fooled by these men is a gullible woman. He would not fool a true man. He would not fool a true woman. But he will fool the gullible. He will fool the infants, the immature. Just as the serpent presented the forbidden fruit to Eve in the garden, so will these deceitful men trick the gullible children, unable to speak the Word of God, into following them. And once we are tricked, he makes us his captives. He makes us his servants. And we are so gullible; we do not even realize we are in bondage. We think they are serving God. But we are:

...always learning and never able to come to the knowledge of the truth. (2 Timothy 3:7)

We are seeking to learn, but we cannot come to _knowledge of the truth_. We cannot come to knowledge of God because we are seeking him through our lust for signs and wonders, not through a relationship with Him. To know the truth, we have to have knowledge of the Son of God. We have to see God in His glory. We cannot seek only the hand of God, but we must seek His face. We must seek to know Him. If we are only motivated by what He can do for us, if we are motivated by our various lusts in our relationship with Him, we will never truly know Him. We will never know the Truth.

> **The power of God is to change lives, not simply to bless the people.**

As long as we remain children, we will be led away by every wind of doctrine. We will not be able to discern for ourselves the truth. We will be at the mercy of these men who through trickery and deceitful plotting toss the people to and fro with every wind of doctrine. If we are only learning what the minister is teaching, every wind of doctrine, or following every manifestation, we never learn to speak the Word ourselves. We will never come into the unity of the faith, the knowledge of the Son of God, the measure of the stature of the fullness of Christ. We will always be held captive to men who through cunning craftiness will keep us in his service instead of preparing us to do the work of the ministry.

Now as Jannes and Jambres resisted Moses, so do these also resist the truth: men of corrupt minds, disapproved concerning the faith; but they will progress no further, for their folly will be manifest to all, as theirs also was. (2 Timothy 3:8-9)

Jannes and Jambres were the Egyptian magicians who duplicated the miracles that God worked through Moses. Just as these magicians worked fraudulent miracles, so will we resist the truth if we operate in the flesh. When we operate in the flesh, we will not submit to the Truth. We will not come into the knowledge of the Son of Man. We will be of corrupt, carnal minds. So, we are disapproved concerning the faith. God does not ordain us to work the signs we are working to gain His approval. That is why Jesus says in Matthew 7:23, *"I never knew you; depart from Me, you who practice lawlessness!"* God never approved of the things they were doing. He never ordained it. He says they are not approved. When we operate in the flesh, we are rejected, reprobate concerning the faith. But there is good news. When we operate in the flesh, we will not progress any further. Sooner or later, we will be exposed for what we truly are. Then our folly will be manifested before all. Once we give up the act, we can fall into our Father's arms and depend on His love and grace and not our own.

All you beasts of the field, come to devour, all you beasts in the forest. His watchmen are blind, they are all ignorant; they are all dumb dogs, they cannot bark; sleeping, lying down, loving to slumber. (Isaiah 56:9-10)

Why is the church open to demonic attack? Why can the beasts come and devour the church? It is because the watchmen of the church are blind. They cannot see what God is doing in the heavens. They cannot see His will for them. Since they cannot see, they also cannot proclaim His will. Their voice has been taken away. The prophets have been silenced so they cannot sound the trumpet. They being "dumb dogs cannot bark." Instead, the church is lying down, loving to slumber. Instead of marching out and fulfilling the will of God, we are lying down, loving to slumber because our watchmen are ignorant.

Yes, they are greedy dogs which never have enough. And they are shepherds who cannot understand; they all look to their own way, every one for his own gain, from his own territory. (Isaiah 56:11)

Instead of being true *shepherds*, they are out to prove what they can do. They are greedy dogs. Paul told Timothy to watch out for those who are lovers of money. *"They are greedy dogs which never have enough."* When we operate in the flesh, we will milk people of everything they have. When they operate in the flesh, they *cannot understand* God's will for the church today. Since they do not understand God's will they *"all look to their own way, every one for his own gain."* They do things according to our own understanding since they have become dull of hearing God's voice. But they are out for their *own gain.* They are out to promote their ministry and themselves. They start to think that godliness is a way of gain. Paul told Timothy *"From such withdraw yourself."* (1 Timothy 6:5) We need to reject this way of thinking and lead the church back to God.

As Christ's body on earth, we have a mandate to free the captives.

"Come," one says, "I will bring wine, and we will fill ourselves with intoxicating drink; tomorrow will be as today, and much more abundant." (Isaiah 56:12)

This *wine* is every wind of doctrine Paul talks about in his warning to the Ephesians. The enemy's strategy is to have us drunk with this wine, never growing into the Head, which is Christ. Then *tomorrow will be as today.* Nothing will change. Satan will remain the god of this earth and the church will not have the weapons to defeat him, being held as slaves by *greedy dogs*. We need to free the saints from bondage to these *greedy dogs*, operating in the flesh.

Freeing the Captives

"I, the LORD, have called You in righteousness, and will hold Your hand; I will keep You and give You as a covenant to the people, as a light to the Gentiles, To open blind eyes, to bring out prisoners from the prison, those who sit in darkness from the prison house. (Isaiah 42:6-7)

We are to open blind eyes. It is blindness to the forces of darkness that is keeping saints captive. We are to open blind eyes, to expose the works of the enemy in keeping God's people in bondage. Bring out the prisoners from prison. God's people are sitting in darkness. They are tossed to and fro by every wind of doctrine. They cannot see. We are to bring them out of darkness. We are to free them from the prison of bondage, manipulation, and control by the deceitful plotting and treachery of the enemy. How do we do it? We do it through the anointing. *"The Spirit of the Lord is upon me because the Lord has anointed me."* (Isaiah 61:1) The same Spirit that anointed Jesus anointed you and me. We have also been anointed to free the captives. We have also been anointed to free those in prison.   How do we do it? By teaching them the good news. We are to *"preach good tidings to the poor."* It is the good tidings, the true gospel of the Kingdom that will free the captives.

As long as we put our faith in man instead of God, we will remain a captive of the enemy. *"But he who puts his trust in Me shall possess the land, and shall inherit My holy mountain."* (Isaiah 57:13*)*   We have to trust in the Lord. Our goal is to possess the land of our inheritance. The goal of the Church is to come into the Unity of the Faith, which is union with God. The goal of the Church is to become the perfect man – Christ in us. The goal of the Church is to be built up into the Head, which is Christ. How do we do that? We have to put our trust in God. *"Seek ye first the Kingdom of God and His Righteousness; and all these things shall be added unto you."* (Matthew 6:33). We have to see Him, no longer being blinded. Then we will possess the land. Then we will inherit the *"holy mountain."* The "holy mountain" is Zion, the New Jerusalem. This is the city of the perfected Church. We will reach it only by putting our trust in the Lord, and not in man.

And one shall say, "Heap it up! Heap it up! Prepare the way, take the stumbling block out of the way of My people." For thus says the High and Lofty One who inhabits eternity, whose name is Holy: "I dwell in the high and holy place, with him who has a contrite and humble spirit, to revive the spirit of the humble, and to revive the heart of the contrite ones. (Isaiah 57:14-15)

The prophet is sounding the alarm: we must build up a highway to Him. We must remove any idolatry that keeps us from coming to Christ - the stumbling stone. God says that if we want to possess this land, His holy mountain, the New Jerusalem, then we must have a *contrite and humble spirit.* The word *contrite* comes from the Hebrew *dakka, which* means crushed, literally powder. Our spirit must be crushed. We have to have reached the position where we can say, like Paul, *"I have been crucified with Christ; it is no longer I who live, but Christ lives in me; and the life which I now live in the flesh I live by faith in the Son of God, who loved me and gave Himself for me."* When we come into this position of humility and submission to the will of God for our lives, to the position of allowing Christ to live through us, then God can revive our humble spirit. It is because our heart has been revived back to its original position in God. When God revives our heart, we can show forth his love, rather than our own. Then God can use us because we dwell with Him.

For the iniquity of his covetousness I was angry and struck him; I hid and was angry, and he went on backsliding in the way of his heart. I have seen his ways, and will heal him; I will also lead him, and restore comforts to him and to his mourners. (Isaiah 57:17-18)

The Lord says that even though we are *backsliding in the way of* our *heart,* He will lead us. He will restore comfort to us. He sent Jesus to free the captives, and now the body of Christ, the Church, will proclaim liberty to the captives and comfort those who mourn in Zion.

God will restore His Church. He will restore pastors and their congregations if they will trust in Him and follow Him.

"Is this not the fast that I have chosen: to loose the bonds of wickedness, to undo the heavy burdens, to let the oppressed go free, and that you break every yoke?" (Isaiah 58:6)

God does not want religious fasting where we give up food, but in that day we oppress, control, manipulate, act with treachery and wickedness by enslaving those we were sent to lead out of bondage. God wants us to free the captives. He wants us to loose the bonds of wickedness and undo the heavy burdens. Everyone kept by wickedness, tossed to and fro with every wind of doctrine, is to be loosed by the gospel of the Kingdom. We are to be taught that we are heirs of God. Everyone oppressed is to go free. No longer will saints be kept in bondage by religious orders, but we are to go free. Every yoke of religious bondage is broken. That is the desire of God, not that we should give up food and continue in oppression.

> **There has to be a genuine concern for the people of God and not a selfish desire to promote a ministry.**

Is it not to share your bread with the hungry, and that you bring to your house the poor who are cast out; when you see the naked, that you cover him, and not hide yourself from your own flesh? (Isaiah 58:7)

God says, do *"not hide yourself from your own flesh."* There has to be a genuine concern for the people of God and not a selfish desire to promote a ministry. We are to *"to share our bread with the hungry."* Jesus is the bread of life. We are to share Him with the hungry. People are hungry to hear the full gospel of the Kingdom. They are tired of being infants (nepios) unable to eat strong meat. We are to share the Bread of Life with them. We are to teach them every thing God has revealed in the scriptures concerning their rights and privileges as sons of God. If they are naked, we are to clothe them with the righteousness of Christ. But too often, we are hiding ourselves from the needs of the people in order to do ministry work of praying and fasting.

What happens when the captives are set free?

Then your light shall break forth like the morning, your healing shall spring forth speedily, and your righteousness shall go before you; the glory of the LORD shall be your rear guard. (Isaiah 58:8)

When the captives are freed, all heaven breaks loose. People no longer in captivity will be able to show forth the light of God to the nations. People released into the gifts of healing, not just the elite ministers, will go forth and spread healing speedily. People will not have to come to church to get healed, but the body will be able to function in the work of the ministry and heal the sick. Y*our healing shall spring forth speedily. Your righteousness shall go before you.*

A people perfected by Christ will show the righteousness of God to the nations. We will not beat people over the head with the Bible and try to force them to conform to our idea of righteousness, but the Lord's righteousness will go before us. People will say, "There's something special about them, there's special peace about them." They will see the glory of the Lord on them and say, "I've got to get right with God." Remember that Jesus already gave us His glory. We just need to be freed from bondage to show forth His glory to the nations. This same glory will protect us; it will be our rear guard. As Isaiah stated earlier, this only comes to those with humble, contrite hearts.

Then you shall call, and the LORD will answer; you shall cry, and He will say, "Here I am." If you take away the yoke from your midst, the pointing of the finger, and speaking wickedness, (Isaiah 58:9)

When we set the captives free, the Lord will be with us. He will answer us. He will be in our midst when we take away the bondage from our midst. He cannot dwell in the midst of bondage, especially when the bondage is done in His name! When the bondage, the yoke, is gone, then He will be with us. When the faultfinding, *the pointing of the finger,* is gone, then He will be with us. Remember, *"There is therefore now no condemnation to them who are in Christ Jesus, who walk not after the flesh, but after the Spirit."* (Romans 8:1) If Christ doesn't condemn us, how can we condemn others? Faultfinding is a demonic weapon. Remember who the accuser of the brethren is. When we practice the fine art of faultfinding, we are acting as his agents, not the Lord's.

We must put away all demonic activity from the church for God to dwell with us. We must put away *speaking wickedness.* We need to put the word of God in our mouths for God to inhabit us. We must quit speaking wickedness - the thoughts and desires of our own heart, the vanity of our own heart - and put God's word in our mouth. Then He will hear us and dwell amongst us.

If you extend your soul to the hungry and satisfy the afflicted soul, then your light shall dawn in the darkness, and your darkness shall be as the noonday. (Isaiah 58:10)

It is when we start sharing the Bread of Life, the gospel of the Kingdom, with those who are hungry for it that our light shines in the darkness.   This will happen when we get the full gospel of the Kingdom into our hearts, that we know who we are in Christ.   Then our light, the light of the Lord, will shine forth from us to the nations. When the Light shines in the darkness of the world, the darkness cannot comprehend it. The Light will always triumph over darkness. This will cause even darkness to appear as noonday. Even when we are down, the Glory of the Lord will be so strong with us that people will be drawn to the Lord.

The LORD will guide you continually, and satisfy your soul in drought, and strengthen your bones; you shall be like a watered garden, and like a spring of water, whose waters do not fail. (Isaiah 58:11)

The Lord will guide the freed captives continually. God will order every step. Instead of bondage and condemnation heaped upon us by controlling   men,   our   souls   will   be   satisfied   and   our   bones strengthened. We will no longer be infants, unable to speak, but we will be strong in the Lord. Rivers of living water will flow out of us. There will be no drought. But there will be rivers of living water flowing from us!

Those from among you shall build the old waste places; you shall raise up the foundations of many generations; and you shall be called the Repairer of the Breach, the Restorer of Streets to Dwell In. (Isaiah 58:12)

This is why it is so critical to free the captives. The freed captives are going to be the ones who build up the waste places. In all those areas that the enemy brought destruction, we shall bring restitution. Even those areas that had been dead for many generations will be restored. There are many truths that were destroyed during the apostasy of the church. These have been dead for many generations. But, the freed captives will reveal truth again to the church that has been hidden for many generations. We will repair the breach. Jesus repaired the breach between God and man through His redemptive work on the cross. The freed captives will repair the breach in the church that keeps us from growing up into the Head.

...but, speaking the truth in love, may grow up in all things into Him who is the head-- Christ-- from whom the whole body, joined and knit together by what every joint supplies, according to the effective working by which every part does its share, causes growth of the body for the edifying of itself in love. (Ephesians 4: 15-16)

The freed captives are going to supply what each joint needs to supply. When we were infants, *nepios*, we couldn't supply anything. We were being tossed around by every wind of doctrine by treacherous, deceitful men who plotted to keep us in bondage. But when we are freed, we can supply that which was lacking in the Body of Christ. By supplying what our joint was meant to supply, we repair the breach, the gap in the body of Christ that was keeping the Body from growing up into the Head – Christ. This fulfills the will of God for the Church – to grow up into the Head, to be perfected, to grow into the measure of the stature of the fullness of Christ.

The Church cannot fulfill its purpose if we are all infants, held captive. So the captives must be freed for the Church to rise up. The captives must be freed for that gap to be filled, for that breach to be repaired. The enemy wants the Church full of gaps and breaches so it cannot fulfill its purpose. So he uses his agent to keep people held captive by demons of fear. They cannot use the sword of the spirit which is the Word of God, because his agents have kept the people infants by using treacherous weapons of the enemy, tossing them to and fro with every wind of his doctrine, not the Lord's doctrine.

When we are freed from the grasp of the enemy, we will repair the breach. The Church will then spring forth in power. It will come forth with all the power of the Lord. Greater works will the Church do then than when Jesus was alive. We will become the restorer of the streets to dwell in.

> **By supplying what our joint was meant to supply, we repair the breach, the gap in the body of Christ that was keeping the Body from growing up into the Head – Christ.**

How beautiful upon the mountains are the feet of him who brings good news, who proclaims peace, who brings glad tidings of good things, who proclaims salvation, who says to Zion, "Your God reigns!" (Isaiah 52:7)

We need to preach this good news. We need to declare to those in captivity that, *"Your God reigns!"* Your God is the Head. He reigns. There is salvation in the Lord's city, Zion, which is the glorified church. When we are freed from bondage, we can proclaim salvation of God. This will free the captives.

Surely you shall call a nation you do not know, and nations who do not know you shall run to you, because of the LORD your God, and the Holy One of Israel; for He has glorified you." (Isaiah 55:5)

When we have been freed, when we have been perfected, when we have been glorified as a Church, then nations shall come to the Church. Isaiah says, *"Surely you shall call a nation."* That is not just a local ministry. The Church is bigger than our own situation. The Church is bigger than our own city. But He has called us to proclaim His gospel to the nations. The freed captives will call a nation we do not know and they will run to us because we are perfected and conformed to His image, because He has glorified us.

6

The Name of the Lord

...but, speaking the truth in love, may grow up in all things into Him who is the head-- Christ— (Ephesians 4:15)

Jesus gave the gifts of the apostles, prophets, evangelists, pastors, and teachers to build the body of Christ up, to bring them to the unity of the faith, the knowledge of the Son of God, the perfect man, the measure of the fullness of the stature of Christ. Then Paul tells us that not only are we built up into the fullness of the stature of Christ, but also we would grow up into Him who is the head – Christ. Isaiah 60 describes this position of the perfected church on Earth. One of the key characteristics is that it was referred to as **"the name of the LORD."**

> **You must walk in Christ's character to walk in His authority.**

Who are these who fly like a cloud, and like doves to their roosts? Surely the coastlands shall wait for Me; and the ships of Tarshish will come first, to bring your sons from afar, their silver and their gold with them, to the name of the LORD your God, and to the Holy One of Israel, because He has glorified you. (Isaiah 60:8-9)

This verse describes people being drawn to the Church in such numbers that they look like a flock of doves returning to their roosts. They are described as coming *to the name of the LORD.* Often when we think of the name of the Lord we think of it as any other name. *The name of the LORD* is the spiritual position of the Church that we are striving for. This is the place in the spirit where the Church has grown up in all things into Him who is the Head, Christ. It is a place where Jesus' character and authority are established in the Earth. Deuteronomy 26:2 describes the church as a *"place where the LORD your God chooses to make **His name** abide."* When we talk about a place where the LORD chooses to make His name abide, we're talking about a place that has His character and carries His authority.

Let's explore what it means to go forth in His name. What does it mean to grow into the very image of Christ Himself? Jesus desires for us to grow up into Him – this is the culmination of the reformation of the Church and will bring about the great revival we are waiting for.

Jesus told his disciples: *"You did not choose Me, but I chose you and appointed you that you should go and bear fruit, and that your fruit should remain, that whatever you ask the Father in My name He may give you. These things I command you, that you love one another."* (John 15:16-17)

According to John 15:16, There are three key prerequisites to be able to ask in the Name of Jesus:

- We must be chosen and appointed.
- We must go and bear fruit.
- Our fruit must remain.

Jesus did not mean that we were to use his Name like a magical incantation to summon up whatever we desire like the sons of Sceva did (*And the evil spirit answered and said, "Jesus I know, and Paul I know; but who are ye?"*). (Acts 19:15) What He means is that we ask from a spiritual position, a perfected position, where we can hear the will of God and are walking in His authority and character.

Chosen and appointed

The first thing we must be sure of is that God has **chosen** us and **appointed** us to do the things we are doing. Jesus said *"Most* *assuredly, I say to you, the Son can do nothing of Himself, but what He sees the Father do; for whatever He does, the Son also does in like manner."* (John 5:19) In order to know what we have been chosen to do, we need to be able to see what God wants to be done. We can only do what God has chosen for us to do after we "see" it. So, we must be, first of all, a prophetic people, able to understand the will of God for our lives. We must be able to discern what God has chosen us for.

Jesus said *"but I chose you and appointed you."* The word appointed is translated in the King James Version ordained. This word is in Greek: *tithemi.* This means *to put into a passive or horizontal posture, to bow, to kneel down, to lie.* So this is not an appointment in a position of authority, but in a position of humility. We must be humble. We must bow down to what God has for us. We cannot go out in a position of our own authority, doing what we want; we must bow to, we must be passive to, we must prostrate ourselves to what God's will is for us. This position that Jesus said he chose us for, ordained us to, appointed us to, was not the governing position under our own authority. It was a position of humility. In this passage He wasn't appointing them as rulers. He was appointing them to a position of laying aside their own ambitions, their own plans, their own messages, their own ministries, their own vision, and prostrating themselves before Him to do His will. And His commandment was to *"go and bear fruit."*

Bearing Fruit

Jesus commands us to *"go and bear fruit."* We cannot bear fruit in any activity outside of God's will for our lives. Before we talk about what it means to bear fruit, let's talk about what it doesn't mean.

Not everyone who says to Me, "Lord, Lord" shall enter the kingdom of heaven, but he who does the will of My Father in heaven. Many will say to Me in that day, "Lord, Lord, have we not prophesied in Your name, cast out demons in Your name, and done many wonders in Your name? And then I will declare to them, "I never knew you; depart from Me, you who practice lawlessness!" (Matthew 7:21-23)

Bearing fruit doesn't mean doing ministry work. After all, they were out doing ministry work. They were prophesying, casting out demons and working wonders in the name of the Lord. If most people were to see them they would say, "They are doing a great work for God." But what does Jesus say to them, *"I never knew you, depart from me you who practice lawlessness."* So, simply doing things we consider ministry is not bearing fruit if God does not ordain it. If God doesn't ordain it, ministry work can be considered lawlessness. Paul described the ministry gifts in 1 Corinthians 12: 27-30. Then he went on to say:

But earnestly desire the best gifts. And yet I show you a more excellent way. (1 Corinthians 12: 31)

The more excellent way is love, as he details in chapter 13.

Bearing fruit isn't prophesying. Paul said in 1 Corinthians 13:2: *"And if I have the gift of prophesy and understand all mysteries, and all knowledge and though I have all faith, so that I could remove mountains, but have not love, I am nothing."* Prophecy is a gift. It's not bearing fruit.

> **The first fruit Jesus requires of us is that we love each other.**

Bearing fruit is not works. Many people think if they work hard, God will honor what they are doing, and then He will honor their requests. They think, "Look at all the things I've done for you. Now, God, I'd like the following things…" Paul said in 1 Corinthians 13:3 *"And though I bestow all my goods to feed the poor, and though I give my body to be burned, but have not love, it profits me nothing."* In other words, *it profits me nothing* means that he wouldn't be recognized for it in heaven. So, if God does not even reward sacrifice of one's own life if it is not done in love, then no other works are the fruit Jesus is talking about.

What is the fruit that Jesus is talking about? Jesus made it very clear in the next verse. *"These things I command you that you love one another."* (John 15:17) The first fruit Jesus requires of us is that we love each other. So, in anything we do, it must be done in love. Whenever we speak, it must be in love. We cannot expect God to honor our requests if we are not bearing, carrying on our lips, love for one another. We cannot slander someone, attack someone, find fault with someone, accuse someone one minute, and expect God to honor our requests the next minute. Jesus makes clear what He expects if God is to honor our requests. We must abide in Him.

If you abide in Me, and My words abide in you, you will ask what you desire, and it shall be done for you. (John 15:7)

We must abide in Him and His words must abide in us. If we are to ask something in Jesus' name, we must ask it in **His** Character, before we can ask in **His** authority. If we do not spend time with Him, if we do not remain in Him, if we do not abide in Him, we will not take on His character. If we don't take on **His Character**, then when we ask things in **the name of Jesus**, but are actually acting in our own character and authority, we are forging the Name of Jesus onto our own desires. We cannot act in our own flesh, in our own desires, in our own will and declare these things in Jesus' name - this is a forgery. *You ask and do not receive, because you ask amiss, that you may spend it on your pleasures.* (James 4:3) We must take on the character of Jesus. This is what Jesus meant by bearing fruit. But how do we do it? We must keep His commandments.

If you keep my commandments you will abide in My love, just as I have kept my Father's commandments and abide in His love. (John 15:10)

What did he command us? *"This is My commandment, that you love one another as I have loved you.* (John 15:12)* God is Love. Jesus' character is Love. This is the fruit that Jesus is most interested in us bearing - that we love each other. But what kind of love are we talking about, but *agape* love. This isn't *eros* love as in between man and wife, but the love of brothers and sisters for each other. We love each other out of our God-given character to love, not from our emotions. Paul explains it further in 1 Corinthians 13:4, *"Love suffers long and is kind."* So, we don't give up on someone the first time they make a mistake, the first time they falter. If we are to love one another, we must also be patient with one another. We must be kind to one another. This is Jesus' character.

"Love does not envy." (1 Corinthians 13:4) If someone has a gift to teach, to administer, to prophesy, I should activate that gift - I shouldn't suppress them and put them in a position they cannot minister to the body in for fear that people won't look to me exclusively in that ministry gift. This is not love - it's envy - and Paul shows us that love and envy do not mix.

"Love does not parade itself, is not puffed up." (1 Corinthians 13:4) Jesus *appointed* us in a position of humility, and if he appointed us in a prostrate position, and he gave us gifts, we should not get puffed up at the manifestation of these same gifts, but humbly submit ourselves to using these gifts to glorify God. The Holy Spirit always seeks to glorify God. If we start to get puffed up, we become like those who said, *"Have **WE** not prophesied in Your name?"* (Matthew 7:22) They were puffed up, caught up at the prophesies that came forth, taking credit for the demons that were cast out by **THEM,** bragging about the miracles **THEY** had performed. They had missed the boat. They hadn't done any of them. When we get puffed up, we forget the God that is behind the manifestation of the gifts of the Spirit. We forget that it is the Holy Spirit working through us. Then we start parading around prophesying, parading around casting out demons, and parading around working wonders. This is not love. This is not bearing fruit.

"Love ... does not behave rudely, does not seek its own, is not provoked, thinks no evil." (1 Corinthians 13:5) We cannot be rude to each other in the body and dismiss it because we are a song leader or a deacon, because we have been given a position of teacher. This isn't doing Christian service. It's doing the enemy's work. Love doesn't seek "its own." It doesn't always look for what's in it for itself - it isn't selfish. If we do things only because we feel we will get

promoted or rewarded, we aren't doing them in love, we are doing them in selfishness.

We cannot be provoked. We must *"bear fruit and our fruit must remain."* Our fruit must remain beyond offense. If we are bearing the fruit of love for one another that Jesus commanded us to bear, it must not depart at the first sign of offense. We must still love each other when someone steps on our toes, when we are overlooked for a position we could have had. If we get offended because we didn't get a position, this is nothing more than seeking our own, being selfish. Love doesn't seek its own benefits. Selfishness seeks its own benefits. Selfishness thinks evil about his brother. But if we love each other, we will pray for each other, not think about revenge.

"Love...does not rejoice in iniquity, but rejoices in the truth." (1 Corinthians 13:6) If we love someone, we do not rejoice when they are doing wrong, even if their ministry is flourishing, even if they are casting out demons and working wonders. If they are practicing iniquity and we know it, we cannot rejoice in, support their works. This isn't love. Even as behaving rudely or being easily offended isn't love, neither is turning a blind eye towards iniquity. Paul tells us to rejoice in the truth. Rejoice when the sin is repented of, not while the sin remains. We must speak the truth in love even when it hurts. We must stand up for righteousness, not rejoice in iniquity. This is what growing into the Head means.

"Love... bears all things, believes all things, hopes all things, endures all things." (1 Corinthians 13:7) We must believe everything that God has spoken to us. We must hope in the things God has promised. This is the fruit of the Love of God that Jesus has asked us to bear. Our love of God and each other must endure all the offenses that will come against us when we follow Him. He sent us to bear fruit that remains, that endures, that bears all things, that believes all things, that hopes all things. Not fruit that easily perishes at an offense, at being overlooked, at not getting the gifts and positions that we desire, but fruit that endures disappointment.

"Now abide faith, hope and love, these three, but the greatest of these is love." (1 Corinthians 13:13) Love must come first. Paul teaches that we can have the faith to move mountains, but if we don't have love, we are nothing. If we are to avoid hearing these words on the last day: *"I never knew you; depart from me you who practice lawlessness,"* then we must obey His commandment – *"These things I command you that you love one another."* They had faith to cast out demons, they had faith to prophesy, they had faith to work wonders, but without the intimate knowledge of the love of God, it profited them nothing.

Our Fruit Must Remain

Jesus told us that we should bear fruit and that our fruit should remain, but remain through what? It is not only petty offenses that we should continue to love each other through. Jesus tells us in John 15:18 - 16:4 that our fruit must remain through persecution.

"But all these things they will do to you for My name's sake because they do not know Him who sent Me." (John 15:21)

What will they do?

"They will put you out of the synagogues; yes, the time is coming that whoever kills you will think that he offers God service and these things they will do to you because they have not known the Father nor Me." (John 16: 2)

> **Our fruit must remain through disappointment, rejection and persecution.**

Who will do these things to us? Those who *"have not known the Father nor Me."* Who is it that does not know the Father? The same ones who go about prophesying and casting out demons while forging God's name to it (without having the blessing of God on it). These are the same ones who will try to murder us through character assassination. This is why God is so harsh on them: not only do they not advance the Kingdom, but they are so confused that they will try to assassinate anyone who actually tries to advance the Kingdom and think they offer God service.

But what does this have to do with bearing fruit? Jesus links these in John 16:1: *"These things I have spoken to you that you should not be made to stumble."* Jesus wants our fruit to remain through persecution. He doesn't want us to stumble at persecution and backslide and leave the Church because we are falsely attacked. He wants us to bear fruit and that our fruit should remain. He wants love to remain. He wants faithfulness to remain through persecution. He wants our fruit to remain through intimidation. If our fruit remains, then He will prepare a table before us in the presence of our enemies. Our cup overflows. We will rule in the midst of our enemies.

But why do they persecute us, why do they intimidate us, why do they try to put us to shame? Because they *"have not known the Father nor Me."* They persecute us when we start to bear fruit, when we start to advance the kingdom.

Our fruit must remain through disappointment. It must remain through rejection. It must remain through persecution. If we bear fruit and our fruit remains, then the Father will do whatever we ask in Jesus' name. Why? Because we will have taken on the Character of Jesus. Jesus endured persecution so that the Kingdom could be advanced. If we endure persecution to advance the Kingdom, we will be acting in Jesus' character. When we put on Jesus' character, we can act under His authority. When we act in His character and under His authority, then we go in **"the Name of Jesus."** Whatever we ask the Father in His name, in His Character, in His authority, in **"the name of Jesus,"** the Father will give to us. When we do this corporately as a Church we start to grow into His image – into the Head - Christ.

There are distinctions between the charismatic move of God and the apostolic/prophetic move of God. In the charismatic, we were satisfied with calling on **the name of Jesus** such that we could "name it and claim it." We would have our petitions heard by God. People would be healed in **Jesus Name.** These are good things and entirely valid. In this season, we are not satisfied with having our individual petitions heard, but our concern is with finishing the work. We are to grow into the Head - Christ. It is to the image of Christ that people will flock to the Lord like *"doves to their roosts"*. We cannot individually grow into the Head. We need to corporately grow into the name of the Lord, so that there is a place created for the flocks of people to come to. Isaiah says this place is created *because He has glorified you.* Paul says that we, the Church, are to grow into the Head – Christ - not an individual growing into the head. This isn't just for one local assembly, one denomination, or even one nation, but the whole Church. The Lord revealed the process by which His end-time Church would be glorified to the prophet Jeremiah.

How the end time Church will be Glorified

"Return, O backsliding children," says the LORD; "for I am married to you. I will take you, one from a city and two from a family, and I will bring you to Zion.And I will give you shepherds according to My heart, who will feed you with knowledge and understanding. Then it shall come to pass, when you are multiplied and increased in the land in those days," says the LORD, "that they will say no more, 'The Ark of the Covenant of the LORD.' It shall not come to mind, nor shall they remember it, nor shall they visit it, nor shall it be made anymore. At that time Jerusalem shall be called The Throne of the LORD, and all the nations shall be gathered to it, to the name of the LORD, to Jerusalem. No more shall they follow the dictates of their evil hearts." (Jeremiah 3:14- 17)

We must be a people that move.

The first step is that we need to move to Zion. God says: *"And I will bring you to Zion."* God is going to lead us out of a condition of backsliding into Zion. So what is Zion, or where is Zion to the Church?

But you are come unto mount Zion, and unto the city of the living God, the heavenly Jerusalem, and to an innumerable company of angels, to the general assembly and church of the firstborn, who are written in heaven, and to God the Judge of all, and to the spirits of just men made perfect, and to Jesus the mediator of the new covenant, and to the blood of sprinkling, that speaks better things than that of Abel. (Hebrews 12:22-24)

In this text, the Lord is clearly identifying the Church as Mount Zion. So, we shouldn't be looking only at the physical Jerusalem, but we should be concerned about the heavenly Jerusalem – the general assembly of the church of the firstborn. This is what the Lord is leading us to become. Our first requirement is to understand in what areas we are falling short of this calling. If we stick with old traditional ways of doing things, they may be good things, but they are not necessarily God's things that will lead us to Zion. We need to discern the mind of Christ for our lives and for the Church.

Being able to see that the position we are in is no longer Zion, but is actually what God considers backsliding, is fundamental. Whenever God has shown us the current position of the church but we regress to a former position, we are backsliding. When God has revealed His way of building a church through love, but we regress back into an autocratic style of leadership based on power and position, we are backsliding. We must return from our backsliding ways to enter the kingdom!

> **Being able to see that the position we are in is no longer Zion, but is actually what God considers backsliding is fundamental.**

As long as we are perfectly satisfied with our position in God, we will stick with our current manifestation of God. We won't even be looking for a better state. We'll think we are in Zion. We'll get stuck in a Pharisee position. We may even embrace an escapist mentality, thinking that God will come and rescue us when we fail to grow into the glorified position He desired for His Church. That's why we have to have a finishing mentality. We can never be satisfied until we've finished the work. Jesus said, *"My food is to do the will of Him who sent me and to finish the work."* That has to be our mindset. As long as we desire to finish the work, we will never get stuck in our present condition. We'll always have a sense of unfinished business until Jesus returns.

This is our first requirement: we must be looking for Zion. Once we start looking for Zion, we need to understand that it will be God who will lead us there, not ourselves. We need to seek out God in prayer continually to discern where the Kingdom is currently located, where Zion is. If we seek His guidance, He already said *"And I will bring you to Zion."*

As important as discerning the mind of Christ for us, we also have to be willing to leave where we are and follow Him. This may mean giving up our own way of doing things. It may mean giving up our positions in the local church. It may mean giving up the ministry that we want to build to pursue the one God had planned. This means starting over according to God's plan. We need to be born again to be saved from falling into a similar Pharisee position, from being cursed to falling into utter obscurity in the Spirit just as Nicodemus needed to be born again to be saved from the Pharisee position he was in. This may mean giving up everything as Jesus asked the rich young man to do. Whatever God requires of us, we must do it if we want to be brought into Zion.

God will Provide Shepherds according to His Heart

"And I will give you shepherds according to My heart, who will feed you with knowledge and understanding." (Jeremiah 3:15)

God promises to give us shepherds to feed us. The next verse says we will be multiplied. In order for us to grow into the Head, as God desires, we must follow the shepherds he sends. The five-fold ministry gifts are the shepherds God was talking about. These are apostles, prophets, evangelists, pastors, and teachers. This is why it is critical to receive the foundation-laying ministries of prophets and apostles along with pastors, teachers, and evangelists, in order to be edified. Through Jeremiah, God says these shepherds will feed us with knowledge and understanding. Paul says they will edify us and equip us.

Apostles and prophets are especially important in transitional times. These foundation-laying ministries give us the knowledge of the design and the ability to build. Without the prophetic knowledge of God's design for the Church, we will build incorrectly. Without the apostolic ability to build, we won't move properly into God's design.

Lift up your eyes all around, and see: they all gather together, they come to you; your sons shall come from afar, and your daughters shall be nursed at your side. Then you shall see and become radiant, and your heart shall swell with joy; because the abundance of the sea shall be turned to you, the wealth of the Gentiles shall come to you. (Isaiah 60:4-5)

Prophetic vision is necessary to be able to see God's plan for the Church. God said through Isaiah that it is when we *see* that we will become radiant, that the glory of the Lord will be upon us. Once we are able to see and become radiant, *then the abundance of the sea will be turned to us*. This represents multitudes of people who will come to the Lord. Isaiah 60:9 points out that they come to **the Name of the Lord**, the spiritual position we inhabit once we have come into the unity of the faith, the perfect man, the measure of the stature of the fullness of Christ. So prophetic vision is key to growing into the Head. We cannot go someplace we do not see. That would be the blind leading the blind. We must see where we are going. It is when we grow into the Head that *"They all gather together, they come to you."*

The people will no longer be drawn to the old manifestations.

"Then it shall come to pass, when you are multiplied and increased in the land in those days," says the LORD, "that they will say no more, 'The Ark of the Covenant of the LORD.' It shall not come to mind, nor shall they remember it, nor shall they visit it, nor shall it be made anymore." (Jeremiah 3:16)

The Ark of the Covenant was where the manifestation of God's glory took place in Moses' time. Similarly, God has manifested His glory in different ways in each move of God. After the Church grows into the Head through the leading of the "shepherds" God gave us, the people will no longer be chasing after old manifestations. In fact, the glory of God on the Church in the perfected position will so far surpass the previous moves of God that the old manifestations of God's Glory will not even cross people's mind anymore. It will fade from their memories. Nothing of that type will be manufactured anymore. In other words, the old manifestations will no longer come to pass. Churches that do not move to Zion, but depend on manifestations to validate themselves, will lose all validation and will become irrelevant in the Kingdom of God. They will become irrelevant like someone looking for God's glory in the Holy of Holies of the old Tabernacle where the Ark of the Covenant used to reside! God says that once we are increased and multiplied, they will no longer look to the Ark of the Covenant. They will flock to **the Name of the Lord.**

All the nations will be gathered to the Name of the Lord.

At that time Jerusalem shall be called The Throne of the LORD, and all the nations shall be gathered to it, to the name of the LORD, to Jerusalem. (Jeremiah 3:17)

It doesn't say, "They are going to be gathered to your church." It doesn't say, "They will be gathered by the signs and wonders." It doesn't say, "They will be gathered to the size of the congregation." In fact, the word says, *"It shall not come to mind, nor shall they remember it, nor shall they visit it, nor shall it be made anymore."* These mindsets about what will draw the people will have to be left behind, just as the Hebrews had to leave behind the manna when they crossed over to the Promised Land. People will no longer visit the cities they used to visit to get a word. They will no longer flock to the same crusades to get healed. They won't even remember it any longer. They are going to come to a place called **"the name of the LORD.**"

Another key difference between the old order and the one that is being established: in the old order, individuals came to the Lord after being attracted to the anointing on an individual. In the order coming, *nations* come to Him. An individual's anointing will attract individuals. A nation's anointing will attract nations. That is why it is so important for the church to be in relationship with each other. A single individual's anointing is not going to establish "**the name of the Lord.**" It is going to be a people in relationship with each other and in relationship with God. This will be the nation of the Church of God. Once David came into covenant with the people of Israel as their king, it is then that he took Jerusalem and made it his city. It is through the same relationships that the Church will establish the heavenly Jerusalem as her city (Hebrews 12:22). Once the church is established in this position, *"all the nations shall be gathered to it."* This is the great harvest of souls that we have longed for. It will come in an abundance that only God could produce, *"and your heart shall swell with joy; because the abundance of the sea shall be turned to you."*

all the nations shall be gathered to it, to the name of the LORD, to Jerusalem

And it shall come to pass that whoever calls on the name of the LORD shall be saved. For in Mount Zion and in Jerusalem there shall be deliverance, as the LORD has said, among the remnant whom the LORD calls. (Joel 2:32)

So, the great revival, the great harvest of souls will come because a remnant people who the Lord has "called and appointed" grow into the Head – Christ. It is from this position that people can call on God's authority, on God's character, on God's name and be saved. Note that the reason that the people can call on the name of the Lord and be saved is because there is deliverance in Mount Zion and in Jerusalem – the Church - among the remnant whom the LORD calls.

Just as Paul said in Galatians 5:22 when referring to the fruit of the Spirit, *"Against such there is no law."* The same principle holds for the Church manifesting the fruit of the Spirit. There is no limit to the number of people that can be saved. There is no limit to the degree of health we can live in. There is no limit to the Glory of God that will be manifested. Jesus said, *"Whatever you ask the Father in My name He may give you."*

Those that come will be established in the Lord.

No more shall they follow the dictates of their evil hearts. (Jeremiah 3:17)

Also your people shall all be righteous; they shall inherit the land forever, the branch of My planting, the work of My hands, that I may be glorified. (Isaiah 60:21)

How many pastors today spend more time counseling their flock than they spend with God in prayer? The question is why do people backslide? Are they just hardheaded, or does their condition only mirror the condition of a backsliding church we are a part of? But Jeremiah says this will no longer be the case for the end-time church to which all nations will come. Isaiah says that the people will all be righteous. They won't backslide any longer. What will keep them from backsliding?

All those from Sheba shall come; they shall bring gold and incense, and they shall proclaim the praises of the LORD. (Isaiah 60:6)

People will bring not only their money, but they shall also proclaim the praises of the LORD. This is because they will not be coming into a body ruled by power, money and position. In those places, people may receive a position based on their gold, their abilities, their knowledge, or their money, not on their position in God. This describes a worldly church. In the Church that has grown into the Head, the emphasis is shifted. They will proclaim the praises of the Lord. The work of their hands will no longer be emphasized, but their praises. Shepherds, not hirelings, will teach them. The plan of the Lord for their lives will be activated. They will step into a position in Christ of true healing, true love, and true acceptance. This they will experience as a result of coming into relationship with true believers who have grown into the Head – Christ.

The reason that God brings this all to pass is not that we can be puffed up, not that we can be elevated. But God will bring this all about in His time so that He is glorified. This is the will of God: **that we grow into the Head – Christ.** From that position we show forth His character to the Earth so that His authority is established in the Earth and He is glorified by it.

7

Every Joint Supplies

For because of Him the whole body (the church, in all its various parts), closely joined and firmly knit together by the joints and ligaments with which it is supplied, when each part [with power adapted to its need] is working properly [in all its functions], grows to full maturity, building itself up in love. (Ephesians 4:16 Amplified Bible)

Paul says that the Church that grows up in all things into the head – Christ – will be one in which everyone does its part. This body grows through edifying itself in love. These people are knit together. This describes the outcome of a Church that is built on solid relationships between individuals in the local church body, different congregations working together in a city and then, national church bodies working together as one global church. In this chapter we will explore how these church relationships can flourish to develop into a body that glorifies and grows into the image of Christ.

In seeing how the global church body – the whole church – grows through building itself up in love, it is sometimes easier to see how this works on the local church level. The same principles will apply to the global church. This scripture says that the body of Christ, like our physical bodies, is joined together by joints and ligaments. In our physical bodies we have joints and ligaments; in the church body, the joints and ligaments are the relationships that bind us together.

In a properly functioning church body, each part is working properly:

- Each person is working – and not idle.

- Each person is prepared for the work of the ministry (Ephesians 4:12).

- Each person has the power – the gifts of the Spirit and the understanding and training in how to use the gifts for the advancement of the kingdom.

- Each person is effective – this requires proper training and guidance by the five-fold ministry to equip and position each worker in his right position to do the work he is supposed to do.

- Each person is supported in his or her ministry work. It is not enough to just train people, but each one needs to be supplied with what he or she needs to do the ministry. This requires allocation of resources from the church. Sometimes this means money. Other times it will be using church vehicles or using the building for meetings.

In this chapter, I would like to explore how a local church can effectively train, equip, and oversee the members such that each one is contributing and is effective in building up the body of Christ, locally, regionally and globally. I will use my home church, Calvary Community Church, in Northwest Houston, Texas, as an example of how this can be done. The church has a three-part vision: 1) To establish people in intimacy with the Lord, 2) To express true Christian Community, and 3) To extend the Kingdom of God in the earth. One can see from the vision statement that the church wants to focus on building up the relationships that form the church (Christian Community) in order to advance the kingdom on a regional and global basis. But all of this is rooted and grounded in intimacy with the Lord. Without Him, we can do nothing that is good (John 15:5). So, before someone commits to doing any kind of work in the kingdom, there must be a solid personal relationship with the Lord. The church stresses spiritual disciplines, like journaling with the Lord, as part of daily devotions to develop and deepen our personal relationship with the Lord.

Training The first step in the equipping process is training in how to minister. The model we use is taken from John Wimber's ministry training model. We call it "Ministry Team Training." The training is usually done on a weekend. We have five modules that each person learns, from the fundamentals of power ministry, techniques for praying on teams, to healing and deliverance. Once someone has completed the first two modules of the training they are qualified to start ministering in the church with others on ministry teams. But everyone is encouraged to complete the rest of the training.

As the name implies, we use a model of ministering in teams. This is important to avoid a "one-man-show" model where the pastor does the entire ministry in the local church. We want the majority of the ministry – mostly prayer ministry – to be done by the members to the members. The idea of using teams is two-fold. In a team you allow a diversity of gifts to be brought to the person who is seeking ministry. One person on a team may receive a word of knowledge about how to pray for the individual. Another team member may receive the gift of discerning of spirits. Another may receive a gift of healing, which the seeker needs. Whatever a person needs, the Lord can supply it through the ministry team that is ministering to him or her. With a team, there is also a possibility of members of the team supervising each other. This reduces possible problems with someone giving advice or counseling instead of praying for the needs of the person. We usually have two to four people on a typical prayer team.

The focus of ministry teams is on listening to the Lord about how He wants to minister to the person. Often a person may come with one particular issue to be prayed for, but the Lord can lead the team to pray in another direction – often getting to the root of the problem instead of ministering only to the immediate need. With a team of people ministering, one member can be interceding and listening to the Lord while the other is praying. In an ideal prayer session, we will see how the Lord wants to minister to an individual and minister accordingly.

When we came to the church, my wife and I had already been baptized in the Holy Spirit and had some experience praying for people. Nevertheless, the training was very helpful in understanding how to function more effectively as a team, how to yield to one another and how to be accountable to one another as team members. There is also some helpful training on prophetic etiquette, as well as practical experience in praying for people in a safe "training" environment.

> **The members, not the pastors, do most of the prayer ministry in the local church.**

A key part of each training exercise is practical training on healing the sick. In most training classes there are about 100 to 150 people from our church, as well as other churches in the area that participate in the training. So there are typically some ailments that people suffer from when they come in.

The first step in this part of the training is to have the trainees listen to the Lord to hear and see what types of ailments He may want to heal. Each person is encouraged to speak up with whatever he or she has heard from the Lord. After we have heard from the trainees what they heard that the Lord is going to heal, we will see if anyone in the group needs healing in those areas. Then teams are assembled with experienced people matched with trainees to pray for those with the ailment. In my experience on the teams, there has always been partial or total healing during these prayer sessions during the training. It seems that God is more interested in our hearts to do His will – to pray for the sick - than in our having perfected some techniques in how to do it.

Practical experience in ministry is a key factor in getting people from theory to practice. The enemy often intimidates people to prevent them from stepping out and praying for the sick. A safe environment where people can "practice" is important. Obviously, everyone in a training class is not expecting trained, polished pastors to be praying for them – so there is grace for the inexperienced to try for the first time to pray for someone who is sick. Also, I have never experienced someone being ungrateful for my taking the time to pray for him or her when they were sick – even if they are not healed. Clearly, people are more grateful when the Lord heals them, but someone taking the time to pray for them blesses most people.

The Bible tells us to pray for each other that we may be healed (James 5:16). Part of building a healthy Christian community is that we pray for each other. We have a saying in the church, "The process is the product." The most effective prayer can be hands-on prayer for each other in ministry teams. This is part of the "product" – the local church. So having people praying on teams is not only important so that the people can be healed, but it is also important in building up the body of Christ in love. Praying for each other is part of building a relationship with another believer – this is one way that people are "knit together." In each of our home groups, we encourage a time for ministry. Having members minister to each other in small group sessions is the primary vehicle for pastoral ministry to be accomplished within the local church.

Gift Based – Passion Driven Ministry Gift Based – Passion Driven ministry is the name we give for our congregation's ministry model. In this model, we encourage people to work in the area of their gifting and passion. The idea is to allow the Lord to lead each individual into the area of ministry they are best suited for. Instead of the church developing programs and enlisting the members to fill the programs, we take the opposite approach. We allow the Lord to speak to someone and give him or her a vision for ministry. This ministry can either be inside or outside of the local church. The intent is that we support ministries that advance the kingdom of God, not to promote the local church.

For example, when the Lord put it in my heart to start a chapter of Ministers' Prayer Network, I submitted the concept to our small group coordinator and pastor. The vision of the group is to pray for the church and encourage and build up the members in their ministry gifting. After meeting with them to discuss the vision and ensure that the church could support the ministry, I was able to form the group. What Calvary does when it supports a ministry is to affirm, bless, and release the ministry. Except in the area of missions, this does not include any financial support.

The typical way to solicit membership in a small group is to have others interested sign up for membership in the group with a six-month commitment. Members sign up for small groups that they have a passion for. People with gifting and desire to pray for the sick join the healing or hospital ministry. If someone has a passion to minister to those in prison, they join the prison ministry. Those with a passion to teach children or youth join those ministries. In this way people are motivated to minister as the Lord leads them, and we feel, in the most effective way. This leads to more inspired ministry and decreased burnout. Passion for what we are doing motivates us to continue even when things are difficult. Instead of doing a job in the church, we are fulfilling the ministry that the Lord has uniquely given to us. With this vision, ministers in the church are also supported in their ministry.

An important part of "being the church" is to see all aspects of our life as our ministry. The Lord is the same wherever we go. If we are working a job, it is also our mission field, just as much as an international trip. We are to be salt and light wherever we go. People should see how we live our lives and it should be a testimony. Part of the practice of releasing people into their ministry is to broaden our minds of what ministry is. It is not just preaching or witnessing, but it is being Christ to someone who needs Him, whether at church, at work, or wherever we encounter them.

Church Support Supporting members as they minister in their area of gifting includes facilitating small groups, oversight of the groups and also support of trans-local and international missions. We addressed the issue of supporting gift based, passion driven small groups above. This is one way that the local church can function, building strong relationships as people minister with those of similar mind and heart, building up the local church, and extending the Kingdom of God. It is also important to support those that have a ministry outside the local church.

Missions are an integral part of the vision of the local church. Most denominations have a missions ministry that the denomination uses to send missionaries throughout the world. One of the negative aspects of the movement to non-denominational church structure is the lack of an organized missions agency. There are some independent missions sending agencies that exist to support missionaries, but they are not necessarily affiliated with most churches. So, it is up to individual churches to raise and support their own missionaries.

Our local church has been of significant support to us in sending us on mission trips. Our primary ministry calling is to teach and preach the word throughout the world. Yet, at this point in our journey, the Lord has us still serving bi-vocationally – with me working as an engineer and my wife as a homemaker. This doesn't give us the time or resources to manage an independent ministry. If we took all the time it requires to administrate a ministry, with all the record keeping, tax filings, legal incorporation procedures, etc., we would not have time to do the ministry work He has called us to. Our local church has helped us to bridge this gap by facilitating financial contributions. When we go on a mission trip, people supporting us financially give through the local church's missions account. The church will also give us part of the financial support we need for the mission. This allows us to focus on the ministry aspect of the trip and minimizes the administrative duties for us.

> **We need to have the humility to understand that none of us has the entire counsel of God.**

Trans-Local Ministry Just as relationships are important in knitting together the local church, they are also important in the city church and global church functioning as one body.

I, therefore, the prisoner of the Lord, beseech you to walk worthy of the calling with which you were called, with all lowliness and gentleness, with longsuffering, bearing with one another in love, endeavoring to keep the unity of the Spirit in the bond of peace. There is one body and one Spirit, just as you were called in one hope of your calling; one Lord, one faith, one baptism; one God and Father of all, who is above all, and through all, and in you all.   (Ephesians 4:1-6)

Behold, how good and how pleasant it is for brethren to dwell together in unity! It is like the precious oil upon the head, running down on the beard, the beard of Aaron, running down on the edge of his garments. (Psalm 133:1-2)

Paul shows us that one Spirit is "in you all." When Jesus prayed for us as recorded in John 17, he prayed that we be one. In Psalm 133, the Lord tells us that there is blessing in unity. There is significant scripture that points us to the fact that the Lord wants us to see each other as parts of the one Body of Christ. I have experienced that a key part of being part of one Body of Christ is to have humility.

We must be humble enough to see others who do not agree with our theology as still part of the same body and able to serve the Lord effectively, even if they disagree with us. I have a unique view on this. I was born and raised in the Catholic Church. When I was in college, I came into a personal relationship with our Lord through a ministry called Search, which was sponsored by my parish, and our priest led the retreat I was on when I accepted the Lord. So, I find it odd when I hear brothers and sisters in the church talk about Catholics as if none of them were Christians. After all, I was saved and stayed in the Catholic Church for many years. Also, I was filled with the Holy Spirit while I was a member of a Baptist Church. Yet many Baptists and Pentecostals want to engage in long arguments about what it means to be filled with the Spirit. It is the same Lord that saved me as a Catholic that saves someone who is Baptist. It is the same Holy Spirit that filled me as a Baptist that fills a Pentecostal. We need to have the humility to understand that none of us has the entire counsel of God, and that more than knowledge and doctrine, he wants us to be one with each other.

The important thing is to bear "*with one another in love, endeavoring to keep the unity of the Spirit in the bond of peace.*" Notice that Paul didn't say, "convince one another of your doctrines," but to bear with one another. The most important aspect of building relationships between each other from various denominations is to come with an attitude of humility and understanding. I have never met anyone who is a Christian that I have not been able to learn something about God from. Each of us has a unique relationship with God and we can all learn from each other.

As I have matured in the Spirit, I have changed some of my theology. One of the situations I was put in helped me to learn this point. My wife and I were leading a "harp and bowl" prayer group at "Love Lines," a Minnesota based crisis phone counseling ministry led by a Spirit-filled Lutheran. The "harp and bowl" prayer model is to combine worship and prayer together. We facilitated the group as prayer leaders. When we started the group, we had a worship leader who could sing and play contemporary Christian music we were familiar with. After a few months, she moved to another city and another sister joined us as worship leader. She came from a Methodist church and was only able to play hymns from her Methodist Hymnal.

My charismatic training had led me to believe that we had to have music that accurately communicated the season we were in, so how could we intercede before the Lord with music that was hundreds of years old? Yet, as we sang many of these hymns by John Wesley, I came to realize that worship was more of an issue of the heart than of the style. If we worshiped in Spirit and Truth, then it didn't matter how old the song was, we could still use it to praise the Lord. An old hymn was just as effective in reaching the throne room as a modern worship song. So, if we keep an open mind, it is easy to see that every Christian has something to offer. Even if they don't agree with our theology, our oneness (unity) with the Lord commands us to be in unity with each other. Breaking this command is just as wrong as committing adultery or murder.

Once we have a group of people trained to minister within the local church, they are also able to join with the citywide church or be sent on international missions. We have used various events to encourage unity within our city. Citywide church leaders organize events to celebrate the national and global days of prayer. It is important that individual churches encourage participation in these citywide and global events. It is through these events that we can come together beyond denominations to express true Christian unity. Another event that helped to unite Houston was Louis Palau's City Fest. Our church joined hundreds of other churches throughout the city to participate in training volunteers as prayer counselors, advertise and pay for the event, as well as attending it.

In these types of events, the church is one body, joined by the various joints and ligaments from individual congregations. But the body is one. It is critical that we come together regularly to remind ourselves of this fact. Otherwise we could start to compete with one another for membership, or compare each other on how great we worship, none of which leads to the unity that the Lord has commanded and prayed for us to have. I am not advocating that events replace true unity, but they do have a place while we are still on our road to true unity and we would not be wise as individual congregations to remove ourselves from these assemblies.

> **Love is the joint or ligament that holds the body together.**

Love The Bible uses many analogies to represent the Body of Christ. It is called a "building" or a "body." Whatever analogy we use, the body is built with love. If competition is the basis of our building, we end up with fragmentation instead of unity. If pride of knowledge is our basis of building the body, we end up with intelligent scholars, but no unity. Love is the cement that holds the living stones together in one building. Love is the joint or ligament that holds the body together.

Without relationships based on love, we can do nothing that is good. Most of the negative stereotypes about Christians arise from quoting scripture outside of the love of God. Even if we have disagreements with other about doctrines, if we have the love of God in us and share that love, we can overcome the differences and still be in unity with each other through our oneness with the Father.

And now abide faith, hope, love, these three; but the greatest of these is love. (1 Corinthians 13:13)

The Church that practices love is the Church that can carry the weight of the revival that God wants us to receive. Because in this Church, when the flocks of people come in, they will immediately come into contact with people who want to see them rise to the position in God that God wants – to fulfill their purpose. That's all they will know. That will be their nature, because they will have taken on the character of Christ and will show forth His glory. The anointing on the people is what will attract the multitudes. They will receive the healing in their homes, not the church building. They will be brought to salvation on their jobs, not at a crusade. Flocking to the Church will be their response after they are saved, so they can be equipped to repeat the process. That is the end result of a Church in which every joint supplies – in which each part does its share. There is no end to the revival that will take place once we truly enter into relationships with each other based on our love-centered relationship with God!

www.ingramcontent.com/pod-product-compliance
Lightning Source LLC
Chambersburg PA
CBHW031326040426

42443CB00005B/237